John Donne

SELECTED POEMS

Notes by Phillip Mallett

MA (CAMBRIDGE)

Lecturer in English, University of St Andrews

LONGMAN
YORK PRESS

YORK PRESS
Immeuble Esseily, Place Riad Solh, Beirut.

LONGMAN GROUP LIMITED
Burnt Mill,
Harlow, Esses

First published 1983
Second impression 1985
ISBN 0 582 78298 8
Produced by Longman Group (FE) Ltd
Printed in Hong Kong

Contents

Part 1
Introduction

The life of John Donne

The life of John Donne is full of fascination for the modern student, for in its mingling of promise and uncertainty Donne's career was typical of his age. He was born in 1572, the third of six children. His father, a successful London merchant, died when Donne was four years old; his mother Elizabeth, a daughter of the writer John Heywood (?1497–?1580), died only two months before Donne's own death in 1631. Both of his parents were Roman Catholics, at a time when members of that faith were coming under increasing pressure to conform to the teaching and practice of the newly established Church of England. Some members of Elizabeth Heywood's family, including her father, went into exile to escape persecution; one of her uncles was executed in 1574; her brother Jasper, a Catholic activist, was arrested and banished in the early 1580s; one of her sons was to die in prison in the 1590s. Donne was later to claim with some justice that no family had 'suffered more in their persons and fortunes' for following the Roman Catholic faith than had his own.

Donne was educated privately at first, almost certainly by Catholic tutors, until in 1584, at the age of twelve, he was sent to Oxford. This haste is understandable. At the age of sixteen all university students were required to swear an Oath of Supremacy, acknowledging the position of Elizabeth I (who reigned from 1558 to 1603) as head of the Church in England. No Catholic could admit Elizabeth's right to an authority also claimed by the Pope, and no doubt many Catholic parents started their sons at university early enough for them to have completed their education before they were confronted with this test of allegiance. Donne was debarred, as a Catholic, from taking a degree. He was probably at Cambridge in 1588–9, and then may well have travelled abroad, perhaps seeing some military service, before returning to London to enter first Thavies Inn and then Lincoln's Inn as a student of law in 1591. Donne was following the usual path for a young man seeking a political or diplomatic career.

London in the 1590s was the city where Shakespeare was about to make his name. It was, then as now, the centre of literary and intellectual life in England, and Donne naturally responded to the excitements of the city. One contemporary, Richard Baker, described him as 'a great visiter of ladies, a great frequenter of plays, a great writer of conceited verses' ('conceited' here means that the poems were intellectually complicated and ingenious). To this early period belong the *Elegies* and the *Satires*, and probably some of the *Songs and Sonnets*, none of the poems printed as yet, but circulated in manuscript among friends. An awareness of this audience of friends is apparent in the tone of much of this early verse, where Donne is deliberately irreverent and unconventional. It is—almost—the kind of poetry that confirms Richard Baker's account of him, as a brilliant young man about town.

Baker's picture, however, is incomplete. Izaac Walton (1593–1683), Donne's earliest biographer, records that at this time Donne was 'unresolved' about his religious position. Donne's difficulties must have been acute. If he remained loyal to his Catholic faith he would have to be prepared to surrender the chance of a successful career, and such a course could not be easy to a young man of the talent and vitality evident in the early poems. The alternative was hardly more attractive: to overthrow his early training, and to abandon the faith for which three generations of his family had suffered exile and even death. Donne rose every morning at four and studied until ten in the attempt to come to a decision which would satisfy the claims of his conscience and his intellect; in later years he could claim to have 'surveyed and digested' all the points in dispute between the Churches of Rome and England. The year 1593 perhaps brought him to a crisis, for in that year a Catholic priest was found in the rooms of Donne's brother and fellow-student, Henry; the unlucky priest was hanged, disembowelled and quartered, and Henry died in prison of gaol fever. Was Donne to see his own life come to so little? His doubts and hesitations are still apparent in the third of his *Satires* ('Kind pity chokes my spleen'), but by 1595, when his mother left her homeland to go into a voluntary exile with her third husband, Donne had probably made the decision to forsake the Church of Rome: at what cost to himself it is now possible only to guess.

In 1596 Donne sailed to Cadiz as a gentleman adventurer with the Earl of Essex (1565–1601) and Walter Raleigh (?1552–1618) in their successful venture against the Spanish, and the following year he sailed again in the less successful 'Islands' voyage to the Azores. Then, in 1597 or 1598, he entered the service of Sir Thomas Egerton (?1540–1617), Lord Keeper of England, as his chief secretary. Sir Thomas was impressed by the young man, and began to advance his career. In 1601 Egerton's political influence saw Donne returned as Member of Parliament for Brackley. At the age of twenty-nine, Donne seemed to have every prospect of winning fortune and distinction.

By the end of 1601 a single act had destroyed these bright prospects.

Since 1596 Egerton had acted as guardian to Ann More, whose father, Sir George More (1553–1632), was later to become Lieutenant of the Tower of London. Donne and Ann fell in love, and were married without the consent of either father or guardian, thus breaking both canon and civil law. Sir George was outraged, and had Donne committed to prison. He was soon released, and Sir George was unable to have the marriage annulled, but Donne was dismissed from his position as Egerton's secretary. Under these circumstances he was unlikely to find another patron, and he and his young wife (she was then seventeen) moved a short distance from London to manage as best they could. Their situation was summed up in a punning epigram: 'John Donne, Anne Donne, undone'.

For a time no doubt they were happy enough just to be together, and some of the *Songs and Sonnets* portraying satisfied love (for example, 'The Sunne Rising') probably date from this period. Sir George was eventually persuaded to accept the situation, and this helped to ease their financial difficulties as their family increased almost year by year. But Donne began to grow restless. He applied desperately to a succession of possible patrons, but was unable to secure a new state appointment. His health began to deteriorate, and he was seriously ill in 1608–9. From these years come the learned treatise in justification of suicide, *Biathanatos*, which perhaps suggests the way his thoughts were turning, and many of the *Divine Poems*. Among these the most memorable are the sonnets known as the *Divine Meditations*, and in particular those in which Donne meditates on the themes of sin and judgement. The cast of his mind was changing.

He continued to study intensively, and possibly put his reading to use by assisting Thomas Morton (1564–1659) in a new bout of polemical writings against the Church of Rome. In 1607 Morton was made Dean of Gloucester, and offered to ensure Donne's preferment if he would take holy orders in the Church of England. Donne, still hoping to find a career outside the Church, declined on the grounds that he was not worthy, but continued to take part in the controversies. In 1610 he published *Pseudo-Martyr*, and in 1611 *Ignatius His Conclave*. He hoped that these works would win the favour of King James, but James too wanted Donne to enter the Church. Donne continued to seek a patron who would help him to some state employment. He already knew Sir Robert Drury (1575–1615), and when Drury's daughter Elizabeth died in 1610, Donne took advantage of the occasion to write a funeral poem for her, published in 1611. 'An Anatomy of the World (The First Anniversary)' pleased Sir Robert more than it did Donne's fellow poet Ben Jonson, who thought its praise of the dead girl blasphemous, and Donne accompanied the Drury family on a tour to France, Germany and Belgium in 1611–12. (According to Izaac

Walton it was before this long journey that Donne wrote for his wife the 'Valediction: forbidding mourning'.) Donne had by now a number of influential friends such as Sir Robert, but although he was again briefly a member of Parliament in 1614, he remained without regular state employment; he wrote in a letter that 'no man attends court fortunes with more impatience than I do'. For a time he hoped to be appointed ambassador to Venice, through the influence of yet another patron, the Earl of Somerset (?1590–1645), but again his hopes were disappointed. He finally surrendered all such ambitions, and in January 1615 was ordained. At the command of King James he was made an honorary Doctor of Divinity at Cambridge; for a time he was a royal chaplain; and then, in 1616, he was appointed Divinity Reader at Lincoln's Inn. He remained there until 1621, when he was elected Dean of St Paul's Cathedral, the post he held until his death ten years later.

In this last period of his life Donne achieved the distinction he had desired for so long, as he became the most eminent preacher of his generation. But these last years too were marked by sorrow and distress. In 1617 his wife, pregnant for the twelfth time in only sixteen years, was brought to bed of a still-born child, and she herself died a few days later. Donne was thus left with seven surviving children to care for, but he never remarried. His own health was still uncertain, and in 1623 he came near to death with a relapsing fever. This illness prompted one of the finest of his religious poems, the 'Hymn to God the Father', and one of the most moving of his prose works, the *Devotions upon Emergent Occasions*, in which work more than in any other is revealed the preoccupation with death which marks much of Donne's writing in the latter half of his life.

In 1630, again seriously ill, Donne made his will, and in February 1631 he preached his last sermon at court, published posthumously as *Death's Duel*. Izaac Walton recorded that Donne's ill-health was so apparent in his voice and manner that those who heard him believed he had preached his own funeral sermon. He continued to prepare himself for death: almost his last act was to design the monument which was to stand over his grave in St Paul's Cathedral. For this he had made a sketch of himself in his shroud, eyes closed and body half-crouched, which he kept by his bed in the last days to remind himself of what he was soon to become. The statue carved from this portrait survived the Great Fire of 1666 and still stands in the rebuilt cathedral.

Donne died, aged fifty-nine, on 31 March 1631. The first edition of his poems was printed two years later. For two hundred and fifty years his reputation as a poet was uncertain, though he always had admiring readers: it is only in the present century that he has been generally acknowledged as one of the major poets in English.

Religious and intellectual background

At the beginning of the sixteenth century Europe was largely ruled by kings, and the culture and the forms of government in England as elsewhere had been largely shaped by the Church of Rome. In 1534, under Henry VIII, England made the break from Rome; by the close of the century it became clear that this break was irreversible, and the extent to which the old culture had given way to new patterns of thought and feeling was already beginning to be felt. With the accession of the Stuart kings, James I and then Charles I, it became apparent that the impetus for change would lead to demands for a new form of government: government, ultimately, by the consent of those governed, instead of government according to the will of the sovereign. Donne was only indirectly concerned with this more narrowly political development, although in 1627 a sermon of his on the duties of subjects towards their sovereigns gave offence to Charles I, much to Donne's surprise. The religious controversies of the century, however, may fairly be said to have moulded both his private and his public life; and, like other major writers of his time, he was aware of and troubled by the shift of thought and feeling which became apparent in the 1590s, a shift from an Elizabethan world which looked back to a medieval past to a Jacobean world looking forward to our own times.

By the end of the fifteenth century there was widespread agreement that the Church in Western Europe stood in need of reform, although the course and character of what we now know as the Reformation naturally varied from country to country. The crucial factor in England was Henry VIII's need for an annulment of his first marriage, and his inability to obtain it from a Pope dominated by his wife's nephew, the Emperor Charles V. The deadlock was broken in 1534, when the Act of Supremacy declared Henry the Supreme Head of a Church of England independent of Rome. The first decisive step of the English Reformation had been taken, and taken, in effect, in the interests of national government. There was no call to the faithful to examine their souls, nor was there any intention to challenge long-cherished ritual or dogma. Henry wanted to preserve unity and stability, and that, he believed, was best done by maintaining as much as possible of the traditional teaching. But individual consciences were stirred by theological arguments carried on elsewhere in Europe by men such as Martin Luther (1483–1546) and John Calvin (1509–64). Soon Henry found himself sending to the stake not only those Catholics who remained loyal to the Pope, but also Protestants who demanded a more radical break from Rome. Had he lived, Henry would probably have been obliged to recognise that the cause of national unity would be better served by more reform than by more burnings.

Under Edward VI, Henry's successor, the reforming party began to establish Protestantism in England. The clergy were allowed to marry, Protestant printers were allowed more freedom, and in 1549 the Act of Uniformity abolished the old Latin mass and instituted a new liturgy as the legal form of worship. These changes were gradual: the English Prayer Book, even when revised in 1552, represented a modified Catholicism, designed to suit a people who disliked foreign authority and wanted a simpler form of worship, but yet did not wish to depart completely from the old ways. But if England under Edward VI was not yet a genuinely Protestant nation the reign of Mary (1553–8) came near to making it one. Mary was an impassioned Catholic, who hoped to undo all that had been done in twenty years of reform, and to re-establish the authority of the Pope in England. With patience and political intelligence she might have been successful, but she possessed neither. In her short and unhappy reign she burned three hundred Protestants, and ensured that her Church would be identified in English minds for years to come with the idea of tyranny.

Elizabeth I inherited a difficult situation. It is impossible to be certain what her own religious ideas were; what is clear is that, like her father, she was determined to secure national unity, and saw the Church of England as one means to that end. A new Act of Supremacy was passed in 1559, the English Prayer Book was restored, and those who refused to attend services in the Church of England became liable to fines. In practice there was at first a measure of religious toleration: Elizabeth had no wish, in her own memorable phrase, to 'make windows into men's souls', and the appearance of conformity was usually enough to secure freedom from persecution. Her Church was designed to be a moderate one; if it gained only moderate support, at least it was unlikely to invite more than moderate resistance. Unfortunately this position proved hard to maintain. In 1569 Elizabeth had to put down a rebellion in the North, which had mainly Catholic support, and another Catholic plot against her was uncovered in 1571. In 1570 she was excommunicated by the Pope, who later let it be known that it could not be thought a sin to assassinate an excommunicated monarch. Elizabeth's ministers were bound to respond by questioning the loyalty of English Catholics. Penalties for non-attendance at Church services were increased, publishing of seditious books was made an offence punishable by death, and Catholic missionaries were expelled or executed. By the end of the reign, about two hundred Catholics had been put to death, nominally for treason, but in practice for their faith.

Elizabeth's Church was also being challenged from within. Many Protestants who had gone into exile during Mary's reign had come under the influence of John Calvin. Calvinist theology held that God had predestined the spiritual fate of every human being. Those whom God had elected were to be saved, the rest were to be damned. There could be no appeal: salvation could not be earned by sincere faith or by upright conduct, nor could it be awarded by the churches. For this black-and-white theology moderation had little to recommend it, and English Calvinists became known as Puritans from their demand that the Elizabethan Church be further reformed, or purified. The Puritans attacked the theology of the Prayer Book, and they also challenged the position of the bishops in the Church. It was this that convinced Elizabeth that they were a 'sect of perilous consequence': it could only be a short step from attacking her bishops to attacking her right to appoint them. From 1583 onwards Elizabeth's Archbishop, John Whitgift (1530–1604), led a campaign against the Puritans, and from the late 1580s Puritan activists, like their Catholic opponents, risked exile or execution.

Both James I and Charles I shared Elizabeth's fears of the Puritans, who were becoming increasingly powerful in the universities and in Parliament, and both gave full support to the anti-Puritan party, known as Laudians after their most eminent bishop, William Laud (1573–1645), in the campaign to establish stricter uniformity in the Church. Under Elizabeth, Puritan objections to the customs and rituals of the Church of England had not been sharp enough to prevent many of them from continuing to worship in it, but the Laudians began to re-introduce into church services and furnishings elements that seemed to the Puritans a revival of Romanism and a betrayal of the Reformation: organ music, stained glass, altar rails, crucifixes. Puritan concern increased when James I sought to negotiate a marriage between the Prince of Wales and a Spanish (and therefore Catholic) Infanta, and released a number of imprisoned Catholics as a gesture of goodwill, while he and his bishops continued to make every effort to check popular discussion of all questions of political or religious authority. In 1622 clergy below the level of dean or bishop were forbidden to discuss the doctrines of election and predestination so important to the Puritans, and clergy of all degrees were forbidden to 'meddle' with matters of state. In 1624 it was made an offence to publish any book dealing with religion or church organisation without official approval. (There is some evidence in Donne's sermons of the 1620s to suggest that his sympathies were with the Laudians in these measures.)

It was becoming clear that these divisions were not to be healed peaceably: the moderation of Elizabeth's Church was a thing of the past. For more than a century, controversy over matters of religious belief and practice had merged with political issues; now, those who wished for further reform within the Church found themselves increasingly committed to a direct struggle against the monarchy. In 1642, just over ten years after Donne's death, England was plunged again into years of civil war.

Significant changes in the patterns of thought and feeling in a society usually make themselves felt only gradually, over a period of several generations. Nonetheless, literary historians find evidence of a decisive shift of outlook and sensibility in England in the late 1590s. The poetry of Sir Philip Sidney (1554–86) and Edmund Spenser (?1552–99) seems to belong to one age; most of the work of Donne, of Shakespeare (1564–1616), and of Ben Jonson (1572–1637) seems to belong to another. A summary but convenient way to describe this difference is to suggest that the earlier writers could accept relatively comfortably what modern scholars have sometimes called 'the Elizabethan world picture', while the later writers, responding to a wide variety of unsettling influences, were unable to do so.

The Elizabethan world picture emphasised above all else the principle of *order*: an order appointed by God and operating throughout the whole of creation. In the natural world the principle of order was understood in terms of a hierarchy, as a continuous 'chain of being' ascending from mere inert matter up to God. The central link of this chain was formed by man, connected by his mortal body to the animals, vegetable life and inanimate matter below him, and by his immortal soul to the various degrees of angels ranged above him. Every link in the chain played some part in the divine purpose, and each was related in some way to man and man's activities.

Man was also to be found at the centre of the universe as a whole, which was conceived as a vast system of concentric spheres carrying the moon, the sun, the planets and the stars, all revolving in orbit around the earth. Here too could be observed the principle of a hierarchical sequence connecting man to his Creator: the various heavenly bodies were supposed to have been so arranged that the substance of which each was formed increased in purity in proportion to its distance from the earth; beyond the outermost sphere lay the entirely pure atmosphere of the 'empyrean', which was the abode of God.

A further principle of order was revealed in a complicated system of analogies known as 'correspondences'. These worked on many different levels: the order evident in the universe was echoed in the corresponding order of the state, where the sovereign was at the centre and each individual was assigned to his own proper social level or 'sphere'; the state in its turn could be seen as an organic unity (called 'the Body Politic'), and so correspondent to man himself ('The Body Natural'); while man could be seen as a little world, or 'microcosm', in which were repeated the same principles of organisation as existed in the whole universe, or 'macrocosm'. The theory of the four 'humours', important in Elizabethan medicine and psychology, is based on this idea of correspondences: just as everything in the universe is composed of different combinations of the four elements, fire, air, earth and water, so each human temperament must be composed of different combinations of the four corresponding humours, choler, blood, black bile and phlegm. The excess of any one of these humours caused ill-health; the remedy was to restore the proper balance, or order.

It was reassuring to believe that the universe was bound together by an infinite series of correspondences and parallels, and this conviction was, understandably, not to be overthrown at once. However, there were a number of factors at work to weaken it during the sixteenth century. The most far-reaching of these, ultimately, was the development of modern experimental science. Medieval and Elizabethan scientists sought to explain natural events by reference to the divine purpose: for example, the appearance of a comet was taken to reveal some disorder in the heavens, and was accordingly interpreted as a message from God to man, a warning to him of some equivalent disorder threatening the human community. The new science, however, was not concerned to illustrate the divine purpose, but to understand the working of natural laws: the appearance of a comet prompted the seventeenth-century scientists to observe its path, and to try to predict the date of its return. In effect, where the old science had allowed religious belief to overlap with rational inquiry, the new science distinguished between them. In making this distinction, the new scientists were necessarily challenging the old conception of the universe as centred on man, and as governed throughout by a divinely appointed principle of order. Two examples will serve to show how great the impact of this challenge was to be.

The first example comes quite directly from the work of the scientists. One of the outstanding achievements of the new scientific methods was to establish that the earth and the other planets revolved in orbit around the sun: this was both literally and metaphorically to displace man from the centre of creation. In repudiating the ideas of earlier theorists, the new astronomers inevitably came into conflict with the traditional teaching of the Church: the old outlook won a temporary victory over the new in 1633 when the Inquisition, acting on behalf of the Church, compelled Galileo Galilei (1564–1642), the greatest scientist of the age, to reject the new theory as heretical. For much of the seventeenth century it remained true, in Donne's words, that 'new Philosophy calls all in doubt', but eventually the doubts were settled, and settled on the side of the scientists. Science, in effect, had won from the Church the authority to define the shape and pattern of the universe.

The second example comes from the writings of Niccolò Machiavelli (1469–1527), which effectively began what we now know as political science. Medieval theorists, accepting the biblical teaching that 'all power comes from God' (Romans 13: 1–6), had limited their discussions to such topics as the divine origin of the state, and the principle of hierarchy within it. Machiavelli simply *ignored* these topics as fanciful and irrelevant: he wanted to analyse the real nature of power in the states he saw being newly forged around him in Italy—states created not by God but by men, and maintained not by an idea of hierarchy but by force and by political cunning. In 1513, in *The Prince*, Machiavelli produced what was virtually a handbook of the ways in which political power could be won and held, and he did so without regard to the question of the divine purpose. He made it clear in *The Prince* that he was aware that he was doing something new: in chapter 15 he explains bluntly that his intention is to 'present things as they really are in fact', unlike those earlier writers who had been content to describe 'imaginary republics and princedoms, which never did nor can exist in the real world'. Machiavelli, it may be said, intended to study political movements in the same scientific spirit as Galileo, a century later, was to study the movements of falling objects.

It was this scientific spirit that Francis Bacon was applauding when he wrote, in 1623, that we are all of us indebted 'to Machiavelli and other writers of that class, who openly and unfeignedly describe what men do, and not what they ought to do'. Bacon (1561–1626) was the most influential English spokesman for the new scientific methods, especially in *The Advancement of Learning* (1605). He argued that soundly based scientific knowledge would lead to technical mastery over the world of nature, and that this would be to 'the use and benefit of man'. Many of his contemporaries were less optimistic. What Bacon welcomed as an escape from the limitations of outmoded patterns of thought, they feared as a challenge to the old picture of the world as orderly, unified, and centred on man. There was, after all, nothing reassuring in the natural world as described by Galileo, or in the political world as interpreted by Machiavelli. Many factors contributed to the mood of anxiety in England at the close of the sixteenth century—the old age of the childless Queen Elizabeth brought with it a climate of economic and political instability—but the gradual breakdown of the inherited world picture seems to have been the underlying cause of the scepticism and uncertainty that characterise so much of the literature of the period.

The fullest expression of this mood of anxiety is to be found in the work of the dramatists. Shakespeare in particular was clearly preoccupied at this time with a sense of the discrepancy between 'what men do' and 'what they ought to do', and in *Troilus and Cressida*

(1602)—a play which may well have been written for the Inns of Court where Donne had been a student a few years earlier—he provided a profound and bitter illustration of the new scepticism. The action of the play takes place against the background of the wars between the Greeks and the Trojans (as described in *The Iliad*, a Greek epic poem from about the ninth century BC). A typical episode is one in which Ulysses, one of the Greek leaders, apparently asserts the familiar Elizabethan ideas of order and hierarchy. In a long speech (I.3. 75–137) he argues that 'the heavens themselves, the planets, and this centre' (that is, the earth) all observe 'degree, priority, and place', and that these principles must be observed throughout the human community as well. If at any point the principle of degree is 'shaked', argues Ulysses, then the whole world will fall into chaos and anarchy. These fine words meet with general approval, but nonetheless they have no influence at all on the way the Greeks conduct the war: indeed, a moment later Ulysses himself proposes a plot which will involve the violation of the principle of degree he has just set forth (the hero Achilles is to be downgraded, and the foolish Ajax advanced in his place). The rest of the action of the play consists mainly of a series of increasingly brutal betrayals in love and war. Not surprisingly, *Troilus and Cressida* has been seen as Shakespeare's dramatisation of the collapse of traditional values—love, honour, loyalty—as a result of the disintegration of the world picture so eloquently described, and then abandoned, by Ulysses.

It would, however, be misleading to suggest that Donne and Shakespeare and all the writers contemporary with them could be divided neatly into those who wholly opposed, and those who wholly welcomed, the emergence of the new sceptical outlook. That the situation was not so simple as this is clear both from the work of the satirists, and from what happened to the love poetry of the period. In each case, poems by Donne supply the most instructive examples.

The sudden fashion for satire in the 1590s was another sign of the changing mood of the times: not only Donne, but also Thomas Lodge (?1558–1625), Joseph Hall (1574–1656), and John Marston (?1575–1634) published verse satires during this decade. The satirists saw it as their task to expose and condemn what Marston called the 'soul-polluting beastliness' of the age (in *The Scourge of Villainy*, 1598), and much of their writing was both bitter and abusive. But it could hardly be said that their work reveals a cowed or defeated state of mind: on the contrary, the satirists responded to life in London at the turn of the century with almost endless energy. Their work abounds in details of manners, fashions and customs, and lively accounts of the disreputable behaviour of courtiers, prostitutes, former soldiers, and (especially) lawyers. The first of Donne's *Satires* ('Away thou fondling motley humourist') possesses this energy in full measure. The poem opens with Donne telling the friend who calls on him that he prefers the quiet company of his books to the noise and bustle out of doors. However, it soon becomes evident that he is delighted to have been interrupted, and his running commentary on all that they see in the streets establishes the poet as far more knowing about the ways of the town than his supposedly 'wild' and frivolous companion. The enthusiasm here for the satirist's task, and the abundance of entertaining detail, suggests that a sceptical awareness of the gulf between 'what men do' and 'what they ought to do' was not necessarily a barrier to a healthy and, indeed, exhilarating appetite for life in all its variety.

The last decade of the sixteenth century saw a renewal of vigour in the love poetry of the age. There had always been many fine Elizabethan love poems, but many more were both competent and dull:

Smooth are thy looks, so is the deepest stream;
Soft are thy lips, so is the swallowing sand;
Fair is thy sight, but like unto a dream;
Sweet is thy promise, but it will not stand.
  Smooth, soft, fair, sweet, to them that lightly touch;
  Rough, hard, foul, sour to them that take too much.

Thy looks so smooth have driven away my sight,
Who would have thought that hooks could be so hid?
Thy lips so soft have fretted my delight,
Before I once suspected that they did.
  Thy face so fair hath burnt me with desire,
  Thy words so sweet were bellows for the fire.

And yet I love the looks that made me blind,
And like to kiss the lips that fret my life,
In heat of fire an ease of heat I find,
And greatest peace of mind in greatest strife.
  That if my choice were now to make again,
  I would not have this joy without this pain.

This poem, published anonymously in 1602, is in the tradition of English Petrarchism, so called after the Italian poet Francesco Petrarca (1304–74), many of whose poems were translated into English during the sixteenth century. This tradition is distinguished by the elaborate and extravagant comparisons applied to the lady, who is as cold and remote as she is beautiful, and to the despairs of the lover, presented as her devoted and suffering servant. Donne's restless and sceptical mind had little use for such a convention, and in the *Elegies* of the 1590s, as in the *Songs and Sonnets*, the traditions of Petrarchism are discarded: in most of these poems the lady is no longer remote, but in the bedroom, and the poet no longer a passive servant but an active lover. The possibility of so natural and desirable a conclusion to their sufferings seems hardly to have occurred to the Petrarchan poets.

The immediate consequence of this dismissal of Petrarchism is that Donne's love poetry shows the same appetite and energy that we find in the satirists:

> Licence my roving hands, and let them goe
> Behind, before, above, between, below . . .
> How blest am I in this discovering thee.

The interest here is very precisely in 'what men do', and not in what ought to be done or felt by the idealised lovers of the Petrarchan convention. In Donne's love poems, as in Shakespeare's *Sonnets* of roughly the same period, the reader is conscious that the realities of human sexual experience are never far away. This is clearly not the case with 'Smooth are thy looks', in which such words as 'peace' and 'strife', 'joy' and 'pain', do not direct us to the real nature of sexual experience, but remain merely words to be shuffled about to suit the symmetries of the poem:

> Smooth, soft, fair, sweet, to them that lightly touch;
> Rough, hard, foul, sour to them that take too much.

Such symmetries are mildly pleasing, and suggest a world that is orderly and harmonious; they belong, in fact, to what has been described above as the 'Elizabethan world picture'. Donne's poetry is of quite another kind, and implies a quite different account of reality. The recurrent theme of the *Songs and Sonnets* is the place of human love not in the timeless and ideal world of Petrarchan poetry, but in a world vulnerable to change and death. In this real world, love may be present under many aspects—promiscuity, hopeless adoration, bitter disillusionment, cheerful cynicism, tender intimacy—and Donne's love poetry encompasses all of these. In this respect, what F.R. Leavis wrote in *Revaluation* in 1936 is still true: Donne is 'obviously a living poet in the most important sense'. Perhaps, then, there is no better way to introduce Donne to the modern reader than to say that it is the peace and strife, the joys and pains, of the world we know that are evoked and examined in such poems as 'The Sunne Rising', 'Love's Alchymie', and 'The Anniversarie'.

A note on the text

The particular selection of poems to which the following notes refer is *The Metaphysical Poets*, selected and edited with an introduction by Helen Gardner, and published by Penguin Books, Harmondsworth, revised edition first published in 1972.

In the early editions, and in the manuscripts, as well as in Helen Gardner's selection, an apostrophe is sometimes inserted between two words even where there is no question of its standing for a missing letter. The device is intended to indicate that the two words should be pronounced with the minimum possible interval between them (for example, in 'The Sunne Rising', in the line 'She'is all States, and all Princes, I', the first two words count as one syllable).

Part 2

Summaries

'Satyre: of Religion'

Donne wrote five *Satyres* during the early 1590s: this, the third, probably dates from around 1594–5. A satire is generally defined as a piece of writing in which vices or follies are held up to ridicule, but only the first part of the present poem is satirical in this sense. The argument falls into three sections: a condemnation of those who fail to seek for religious truth (lines 1–42); encouragement to seek 'true religion' despite the doubts and conflicts of an age of religious controversy (lines 43–87); and a warning that it is better to risk persecution for disobeying the secular authorities, than to risk damnation by betraying the truth reached by the efforts of the individual conscience. For the background to the poem, see the second section of the Introduction.

It is sometimes suggested that Donne learned his poetic skills from the example of the London theatres, but in some parts of this poem the verse is handled with a freedom and assurance that was not to be heard on the stage until the end of the 1590s.

NOTES AND GLOSSARY:

Kinde pitty . . . /Those teares to issue: the 'sins' he is about to consider demand his pity for those who are his fellow human beings, but they also provoke his contempt, so that the two impulses check each other

be wise: the wise course is neither to laugh at sins nor to weep over them

railing: abusing, speaking scornfully

worne maladies: faults which have been present for a long time

the first blinded age: the age of pagan philosophy, before the light of the Christian revelation

Are not heavens joyes . . . earths honour was to them?: can the promise of bliss in heaven not calm our desires, as the hope of honour on earth calmed those of the pagan philosophers?

As wee do them in meanes . . . /Us in the end: we have the advantage over the pagans in possessing the means of getting to heaven (the Christian revelation); may they nonetheless surpass us in achieving the end, and getting there, while we fail and go—elsewhere?

whose merit/Of strict life may be imputed faith: the merit of their virtuous lives may be allowed to make up for the faith they necessarily lacked, but which was otherwise necessary for salvation. See the note on 'imputed grace' in 'Elegie: To his Mistris Going to Bed' below

so easie wayes and neare: such easy and direct ways

ayd mutinous Dutch: at the end of the sixteenth century a number of English soldiers went to assist the Dutch in their war against the Spanish

leaders rage: the unpredictable temper of a military commander

dearth: famine, shortage of supplies

frozen North discoveries: the known existence of a south-west passage into the Pacific led sixteenth-century explorers to seek a corresponding north-west route

Salamanders: lizard-like animals supposed to be able to live in or endure fire

like divine/Children in th'oven: in the Old Testament story Shadrach, Meshach and Abednego walked unharmed in the fiery furnace into which they were thrown by Nebuchadnezzar, the king of Babylon (see Daniel 3)

fires of Spain: the Spanish Inquisition handed over heretics to be burned; those who fought against them for the Dutch would be considered heretics

and the line: the heat of the equator (the 'line')

limbecks: alembics, used in distilling (a process which requires the use of great heat)

must every hee/ . . . words?: must every person who will not hail your mistress as a goddess draw his sword to fight, or else endure your insults and abuse?

and his: and God's

Sentinell: soldier on guard duty

forbidden warres: wars whose purposes are merely worldly

appointed field: the moral battle-ground, where every Christian was required to fight on God's side against the forces of evil

The foule Devill . . . his whole Realme to be quit: the devil would gladly surrender his whole kingdom of Hell to you, but out of hate rather than love, in order to rid himself of it

The worlds all parts: all the parts of the world

the worlds selfe: the world itself

in her decrepit wayne: the world was believed to be in its wane, that is, running down

last: finally
Flesh (it selfes death): the flesh is the cause of its own death, because the sins of the flesh lead to death
Mirreus: myrrh gives incense its smell. Mirreus is therefore the man who loves incense, which was used in the Roman Catholic Church
unhous'd here: rejected here, in Protestant Britain
her ragges: the few scraps of the original truth still recognised by the Roman Church
wee here obey/The statecloth: in England it was the custom to bow to the throne even when the monarch was not present
Crantz: presumably chosen as a representative German-sounding name, the Reformation movement having begun in Germany
brave: ostentatious, showy. The Roman Church used a more elaborate form of ritual than the Reformed churches
inthrall'd: enslaved, won over
Geneva: Geneva was the home of the Puritan John Calvin (1509–64), and was organised along rigorously Protestant lines
yong: the Protestant churches belonged to the sixteenth century whereas the Church of Rome claimed to go back to Christ's disciple, St Peter
Lecherous humors: tastes in lechery
wholsome: attractive
drudges: working girls
Graius: a Greek. It is not clear why Donne chooses the name
ambitious bauds: ambitious pimps, paid for procuring lovers for their mistress, and therefore willing to say anything in her praise, however false or exaggerated
lawes/Still new like fashions: a number of laws were passed to regulate religious practice during the reign of Elizabeth I
is onely perfect: is the only perfect one
imbraceth: embraces, chooses
Godfathers: spiritual guides
tender to him: offer to him
being tender: while or because he is weak and young
as Wards still/... Pay valewes: as wards accept the marriage arranged for them by their guardians, or else pay a fine. Elizabeth's Act of Uniformity (1559) imposed fines on recusants, that is, on those who refused to attend the parish church

Carelesse: unconcerned

Phrygius: a Phrygian, from the ancient country of Asia Minor. It is not clear why Donne chooses the name

Graccus: member of the Roman family of that name. Donne perhaps uses it because in the second century BC several members of the family were distinguished for their personal integrity and desire to act justly

all as one: equally

divers habits: different costumes

one kinde: of one species

So doth, so is Religion: religion may appear in different forms in different countries, but is in fact everywhere one and the same

this blind-/nesse too much light breeds: believing that every religion has the light of truth, he is blinded to the point where he cannot distinguish true from false

unmoved: dispassionate, not easily led astray by momentary feelings

Of force must one, and forc'd but one allow: you must necessarily admit one religion as the true one, and even under pressure must not admit any other as true

aske thy father . . . a little elder is: Donne is referring to the words of Moses to the people of Israel: 'Ask thy father, and he will shew thee; thy elders, and they will tell thee' (see the Bible, Deuteronomy 32:7). The suggestion is, that it is necessary to recover the original truth, which was once revealed but has now been obscured or forgotten

Hee's not of none, nor worst, that seekes the best: the man who pauses to seek the true religion is not a man of no religion, nor of the worst religion. At the time he was writing this poem Donne was, according to Walton, 'unresolved what religion to adhere to'

To adore, or scorne an image, or protest: to be a Roman Catholic, an anti-Catholic, or a Protestant

in strange way/To stand inquiring right: to pause when one is lost to consider which is the right road

To sleepe, or runne wrong, is: to give up the search, or to choose too hastily, is certainly the way to go wrong in the end

Cragged: steep, rugged

about must, and about must goe: must travel by a gradual and round-about path in order to make his way

suddennes: steepness

rest: make its final choice

none can work in that night: from the New Testament: 'the night cometh, when no man can work' (see John 9:4)

To will: to be going to, to consider this as a task for the future

Hard deeds . . . indeavours reach: hard deeds are done through hard physical work, and hard knowledge is gained through strenuous mental effort

mysteries . . . to all eyes: we cannot help seeing the sun, even though we cannot look at it directly; in the same way we know that there are religious truths, or 'mysteries', even though the mind cannot comprehend them fully

men do not stand/ . . . hangmen to Fate: our situation is not so desperate that God has given the authorities a free hand to persecute just as they wish; they are merely the instruments of Fate, carrying out the will of God and not their own

let thy Soule be tyed/To mans lawes: allow your choice of religion to be made for you by man-made laws

boot thee: do you any good

Philip . . . Gregory/A Harry, or a Martin: Philip II of Spain, a deeply Catholic monarch; Gregory XIV, the then Pope; Henry VIII, the founder of the English Church; Martin Luther (1483–1548), who published in 1517 his *Ninety-five Theses upon Indulgences*, sometimes said to have begun the Reformation

Is not this excuse . . . /Equally strong?: will this excuse not serve equally well for opposite religious groups?

That thou mayest . . . is idolatrie: it was widely agreed throughout the sixteenth century that the secular authorities were entitled to require a certain measure of obedience, but that there was a limit to what could be demanded; to exceed that limit was to change a proper authority into tyranny. The question of where the limit was, was endlessly debated, and Donne is not really providing an answer

As streames are, Power is . . . in the sea are lost: the argument is, that all power comes from God (the 'calme head' or source). Some authorities rule in accordance with God's laws, and those who obey these authorities will prosper: some other authorities (likened here to a stream at a distance from the calm source) ignore God's will, and those who allow themselves to be driven by these godless authorities will be destroyed

Three *Elegies*

In Helen Gardner's major edition of Donne's love poetry fourteen poems are printed as *Elegies*. In modern usage the term is generally reserved for poems of lamentation for the dead, but in the sixteenth and seventeenth centuries it could be applied to almost any reflective poem written in a regular metre (in Donne's case, rhyming couplets). Donne's *Elegies* belong to the mid-1590s, and probably owe their inspiration to the *Amores*, or love poems, of the Roman poet Ovid (43 BC–AD 18). One main tradition of sixteenth-century love poetry was the Petrarchan one, so named after the early Italian poet Francesco Petrarca (1304–74), whose poems often provided the model for English imitations. In this tradition the woman addressed is idealised, and the lover is cast in the role of a suffering (and often complaining) servant. The Ovidian tradition, on the other hand, was realistic, dramatic and direct, and no doubt appealed to Donne precisely because of its non-Petrarchan character. Five of the *Elegies*, including 'On his Mistris' and 'To his Mistris Going to Bed', were evidently considered too direct, and the licenser, or censor, refused permission for them to be printed in the first edition of Donne's poems in 1633.

'Elegie: His Picture'

NOTES AND GLOSSARY:

take my Picture: presumably a miniature portrait of himself

but I dead: when I am dead

shadowes both: the word 'shadows' could be applied to ghosts, and to images or portraits

rude: clumsily constructed

hairecloth: coarse cloth made of hair

With cares rash sodaine hoarinesse o'rspread: when stress and hardships have turned his hair prematurely grey

powders blew staines: blue gunpowder stains

taxe thee: criticise you, demand an explanation from you

foule: ugly

reach: affect. She will not be harmed by any of the changes in his appearance

That which in him . . . seemes tough: the comparison is between milk for babies and meat for adults. He suggests that if she is challenged to defend her choice of him, she will explain that while her young love was indeed fed by his outward beauty, her more mature love is able to be nourished by her sense of the whole man. Those with less experience of love would be unable to manage this mature response

'Elegie: On his Mistris'

NOTES AND GLOSSARY:

strange: when they were strangers to one another
fatall: significant, momentous
interview: meeting
remorse: pity, compassion
Begot: created
want and divorcement: want of each other, and separation
I conjure thee: I solemnly beg you
to seal joint constancie: to guarantee our fidelity to each other
Temper: moderate, calm down
impetuous rage: excited and over-hasty passion
feign'd: pretended, disguised
onely worthy . . . /Thirst to come back: only you could create and develop in me a longing to return
else: otherwise
Boreas: in Greek mythology, the god of the North wind
Thou hast read/ . . . hee lov'd: the myths in fact tell how Boreas carried Orithea away when her father refused them permission to marry, but not that she came to any harm as a consequence
Fall ill . . . /Dangers unurg'd: whether the outcome is fortunate or not, it is madness to endure dangers not forced upon them
Feede on this flatterye: believe this fiction, that is, console yourself by believing what you know is untrue
Dissemble nothing: do not pretend anything, or disguise yourself in any way
not a boy: do not pretend to be a boy
nor change/Thy bodies habit, nor mindes: do not change your clothes, or alter your mind
bee not strange/To thy selfe onely: if she disguised herself as a boy, she would feel strange to herself, and everyone else would immediately see through the disguise
as soone/Ecclips'd as bright: the moon is still the moon, whether shining brightly or in eclipse
Camelions: chameleons, reptiles which are able to change the colour of their skin to suit their surroundings
Spittles: hospitals, especially those for the treatment of venereal diseases. Syphilis was known as the 'French disease'
Loves fuellers: those who deliberately encourage passion in themselves

Players: actors were generally associated with an immoral way of life

knowe thee,'and knowe thee: see through your disguise, and sexually possess you (the verb 'to know' was commonly used for sexual coition)

Th'indifferent Italian: the Italian is here assumed to be equally willing to ravish either a boy or a girl, so her disguise will still not protect her. It was presumably this passage which made the licenser uneasy

As Lots faire guests were vext: in the Old Testament story Lot entertained two angels in his house in Sodom, but the Sodomites supposed them to be two beautiful young men, and demanded to be allowed to ravish them (see Genesis 19)

spongie hydroptique: drunken (hydropsy, or dropsy, is a disease associated with an insatiable thirst)

displease: harm, distress

England is only'a worthy gallerie: England is the only proper gallery for her. The ante-room used for those waiting to see the sovereign was called a gallery

Our greate King: God

blesse, nor curse/Openly loves force: do not speak in public of the power of love, either to praise it or to complain of it

midnights startings: nightmares

Assayld: attacked

Augure mee better chance: he does not wish her fears for his safety to be an ill omen, predicting harm to him

except: lest, in case

enough: that is, enough happiness, or good 'chance'

'Elegie: To his Mistris Going to Bed'

The most satisfactory parts of this poem are probably those which most freely express the poet's sexual desire, as he watches his mistress undress for bed. The legal and theological imagery seems to be present less because it is appropriate to this particular poem (and if, as the opening lines perhaps suggest, the lady is a prostitute, the imagery is definitely *in*appropriate), than because Donne wished in a general way to mock the more solemn Petrarchan poems of his time.

NOTES AND GLOSSARY:

all rest my powers defie: his powers, or sexual energies, prevent him from settling down to rest

I in labour lye: he waits impatiently, as a woman in labour awaits the delivery of her baby

The foe . . . the foe: the male and female sexual organs, imagined as waiting to join battle

standing: keeping erect and ready

heavens zone: the outermost sphere of the universe carried the fixed stars, which would appear like a belt across the heavens

spangled brest-plate: the stomacher, that is, the front-piece of a dress, covering the breast and the pit of the stomach, and often decorated with jewels

busy: prying, intruding

harmonious chime: she is wearing a chiming watch

that happy buske . . . stand so nigh: he envies her corset, which, stiffened with whalebone, can remain stiff indefinitely, even though so close to her. He begins to fear that he might not be able to match it. See note on 'standing' above

steales: goes quietly away

coronet: a metal band worn around the forehead

dyadem: diadem, or head-band, often decorated with jewels

Mahomets Paradise: a heaven made up of entirely sensual pleasures

and though/Ill spirits walk in white: even if evil spirits disguise themselves by wearing white garments

these Angels: women

They set our haires, but these the flesh upright: this is a third joke about the male erection. Evil spirits only make the hair stand on end (through fear)

safeliest when with one man man'd: most safe when inhabited or possessed by one man only

Empiree: the territory owned by an emperor

bonds: commitments, or more simply, her arms. Donne probably has in mind the familiar Christian idea, that perfect freedom is only to be found in the service of Christ

where my hand is set my seal shall be: he has put his hand on her as if signing a contract between them (compare 'bonds' in the previous line), and he will now consummate their love, as if confirming a contract with the imprint of his seal

As soules unbodied . . . whole joyes: as souls must free themselves of their bodies in order to taste the joys of heaven, so lovers' bodies must be free of their clothes to gain the fullest bliss

Atalanta's balls, cast in mens viewes: in the story by Ovid, Atalanta would only marry a man who could beat her in a foot-race. Hippomenes distracted her by throwing three golden balls down in front of her, and so won the race. Donne rather muddles his comparison by having *men* fall victim to the strategies of *women*

theirs: what merely belongs to them

laymen: the uneducated majority, who are quite content to admire the outward show, such as a woman's jewelry or the bright covers of a book, and so fail to appreciate the greater value of the woman herself, or the book's contents

mystique: mystic, containing secrets which only the dedicated few will be able to discover

imputed grace: Donne is here borrowing an idea from the theology of Calvin. Calvin argued that men were unable to win salvation through any merit of their own, but a few were chosen by God to be saved because the righteousness or 'grace' of Jesus Christ was 'imputed' or credited to them: that is, they were saved for merits which were not strictly their own. Donne is suggesting that no man deserves the joy he longs for with a woman, but can only hope that the woman will impute to him her own infinitely superior qualities, and love him for them

liberally: freely, unreservedly

Here is no pennance, much lesse innocence: the colour white was associated with penitence and with virginity; the lady of this poem, therefore, has no reason to keep on her white nightgown

more covering than a man: there are two meanings here: (*a*) more covering than the poet himself is wearing; (*b*) anything else to cover her than a man

From the *Songs and Sonnets*

The second edition of Donne's poems (1635) collected together a group of love lyrics as *Songs and Sonnets*, although only six of the poems are 'songs' in the sense that they were written to fit existing tunes, and none of them are formally sonnets (that is, poems fourteen lines in length). Helen Gardner's major edition of the love poetry prints fifty-four poems as *Songs and Sonnets*. None of them can be dated with certainty, although Helen Gardner argues for a distinction between an earlier group (written before 1600), and a later group (written after

1602). The range and strength of feeling exhibited in these poems reveal Donne as a love-lyricist of the very highest order, and most modern readers would regard the *Songs and Sonnets* not only as Donne's major achievement, but also as one of the major achievements of English poetry.

'The Flea'

The flea provided a popular subject for love poetry throughout Europe in the sixteenth century, following a medieval poem then attributed to the Roman poet Ovid. The poet usually envied the flea its freedom on his mistress's body, or its death at her hands while in the ecstasy of its contact with her. By having the flea bite both him and his mistress, Donne discovers a variation on the motif.

NOTES AND GLOSSARY:

Marke: observe

our two bloods mingled bee: sexual intercourse was believed to be the mingling of the blood of each of the partners

this enjoyes before it wooe: the flea is satisfied without the trouble of a long courtship

pamper'd: over-indulged

one blood made of two: see the note on 'our two bloods' above

grudge: complain, express reluctance

cloysterd: a cloister is a covered walk in a religious building, for example, in a monastery. The flea is seen here as a temple in which their marriage has taken place

Jet: a deep glossy black

Though use make thee apt to kill mee: though she is in the habit of killing him (by her refusal of him)

three sinnes in killing three: murder and suicide because the blood of both is included in the flea, and sacrilege because as a temple the flea is now a holy place

sodaine: (here) violent

Purpled: stained with blood in killing the flea. In grand drama blood was often said to be purple

Yet thou triumph'st . . . tooke life from thee: the lady argues that in killing the flea she has demonstrated the poet's arguments to be ridiculous, for no harm was done and no sins were committed. He turns her triumph against her by claiming that there will be no harm done or sin committed when she eventually yields to him

'The Good-Morrow'

This brief but complex poem is organised around two central metaphors, of a pair of lovers 'waking' into a new life together, and of the new 'world' created by their mutual love. Neither image was original to Donne: what makes the poem so characteristic is that the images are not used merely decoratively, to give poetic status to a simple idea, but argumentatively, to reveal more about the experience of love than was at first evident.

NOTES AND GLOSSARY:

by my troth: truly

were we not wean'd till then?/ . . . childishly?: the suggestion is that they have now passed together from the clumsy and immature sexual experiences of their past, into a more sophisticated and adult awareness. There is probably an indecent pun on 'countrey', as there is when Hamlet speaks of 'country matters' in Shakespeare's play (*Hamlet*, III.2.112)

snorted: snored

seaven sleepers den: the cave in which seven young Christians from Ephesus were walled up alive as they attempted to escape persecution by the emperor Decius. They awoke 187 years later to find that Christianity was now the officially accepted religion

But this, all pleasures fancies bee: all other pleasures except this of their love are mere fancies

If ever any beauty . . . a dreame of thee: the other beautiful women he had seen, desired, and possessed as mistresses, were only shadows or images of the reality he now finds completely expressed in her

good morrow: the usual Elizabethan greeting; good morning. The lovers are waking up in bed together

For love, . . . controules: true love removes the restless desire to see other people or places

one little roome, an every where: an idea to which Donne often returns, notably in 'The Sunne Rising'

Let sea-discoverers . . . worlds on worlds have showne: the two lovers refuse to be interested in the new worlds, or continents, discovered by explorers, or in the unexplored worlds revealed in the new maps of the heavens

Let us possesse . . . and is one: let us possess our world of mutual love; you are the world to me, as I am the world to you

My face . . . appeares: as implied in 1.10, they are gazing at each other

plaine: honest, undisguised

Where can we finde . . . declining West?: her eye reflecting him, and his eye reflecting her, suggest the two hemispheres or half-worlds, which together make up one world. But each hemisphere is special, or privileged: there is no cold Northern region, and no Western sunset leading on towards night. It would of course be impossible to construct a sphere consisting only of the South and the East; the logic is illusory, and Donne expects us to recognise this

What ever dyes, was not mixt equally: alluding to the medieval and Elizabethan idea that decay and corruption result from the lack of perfect balance and proportion in the elements of which all bodies are constituted

If our two loves . . . none can die: variant readings in the manuscripts suggest that Donne himself was not certain how to finish this poem. The sense is this: Whatever dies or decays does so because of some lack of balance or unity. If we really are one world, or if at any rate our two loves are so exactly matched that there can be no decay, then there can be no death of love

'Song: Goe, and catch a falling starre'

Poems based on a list of impossible tasks were and are quite common, at both the sophisticated and the popular level. Here the ultimate impossibility is to find a woman who is both chaste and beautiful.

This poem is one of those said in some manuscripts to have been written to fit existing tunes.

NOTES AND GLOSSARY:

a mandrake roote: the mandrake has a forked root, and was believed to resemble the human form

who cleft the Divels foot: the Devil was popularly supposed to have a cleft, or divided, hoof

Mermaides: mermaids are imaginary sea-creatures, with the face and body of a woman, but the tail of a fish. They are often associated with song

to keep off envies stinging: to protect myself from the attacks of jealous people

What winde/ . . . honest minde: the suggestion is that honesty will never help one to advancement or promotion. The rhymes here (find – wind – mind) were correct until the eighteenth century

If thou beest borne to strange sights: if you were born with the gift of second sight (which enables you to see 'things invisible' to others)
snow: here used as a transitive verb: turn your hair white
befell thee: happened to you
last: remain true and chaste

'The Undertaking', or 'Platonic Love'

Donne claims in this poem to have achieved an entirely spiritual love, completely free from sensual desire. The Greek philosopher Plato (*c.* 427–348 BC) described such love, notably in his work *The Symposium*.

NOTES AND GLOSSARY:
braver: finer
the Worthies: the Nine Worthies were nine great warriors, ranging from the legendary Hector of Troy in ancient times to the medieval Godfrey of Boulogne, who were occasionally brought on stage, as in Shakespeare's *Love's Labour's Lost* (V.2.), to boast of their great deeds. Donne exceeds them both in achievement and in modesty
It were but madnes . . . can finde none: it would be pointless nowadays to teach anyone the skill of cutting specular stone, since there is none left to be cut. 'Specular stone' was a stone supposedly used in ancient times to build temples with transparent walls, but no longer available in Donne's time
Loves but their oldest clothes: loves only the outward physical form, seen as the old clothes of the inner, spiritual self
though placed so: although it is a love of this high and rare kind
prophane men: men who would be contemptuous or incredulous of sacred matters. Donne often uses the idea of love as a religious mystery, which he and his lady can understand, but which is hidden to the 'prophane' or the 'laity'. See, for example, 'Valediction: forbidding mourning' (ll 7–8), and the whole argument of 'The Canonization' and 'The Extasie'

'The Sunne Rising'

Poems in which lovers respond to the dawn, known as *aubades*, are very common: this is one of the most attractive of them, and one of the most popular of Donne's poems. In it he both celebrates a fulfilled and happy love, and develops further a favourite theme, of two lovers making up one world.

NOTES AND GLOSSARY:

Busie: interfering

unruly: disorderly

Must to thy motions lovers seasons run?: must lovers adapt themselves to your time-keeping?

pedantique: fussy, inclined to insist over-much on trivial matters (here, that it is morning)

sowre prentices: ill-tempered apprentices

the King will ride: King James was an enthusiastic huntsman, which obliged his attendants to get up early. The reference dates the poem as after 1603, when James came to the throne (and also, therefore, after Donne's marriage in 1601)

Call countrey ants to harvest offices: summon industrious farm-labourers to the duties of harvesting

all alike: unchanging

rags of time: the usual divisions of time are seen as tattered clothing, in comparison with the timeless world of their love

reverend: deserving respect

both the'India's of spice and Myne: the East Indies (India) provided spices, the West Indies gold

play us: imitate us

All honor's mimique; All wealth alchimie: this is the only true honour and wealth; all else is a false pretence (alchemy: the science which tried unsuccessfully to turn base metals into gold)

Thine age askes ease: the sun, being so old, needs to lead an easier life than before

This bed thy center is, these walls, thy sphere: this bed is the centre of the universe, and the walls of the room mark the new path of the sun's orbit around the centre

'The Canonization'

An elaborately argued poem in which the poet first suggests that he and his lady are not important enough to deserve the world's critical attention, and then changes his ground to claim that, as martyrs brought to death by their love, they will be seen as supremely important by future generations of lovers.

NOTES AND GLOSSARY:

Or . . . or: either . . . or

chide: mock

palsie: physical shakiness associated with old age

Arts: studies

Take you . . . a place: pursue a career, obtain a position at court

Observe . . . his grace: seek favour with some nobleman or bishop

the Kings reall . . . /Contemplate: either gaze at the King's real face (that is, seek to become a court favourite), or at the stamped face on his coins (that is, seek to acquire wealth). The reference to the King dates this poem as after 1603

what you will, approve: do whatever you like

So: so long as, provided that

my sighs: in lines 10–15 Donne mocks the sufferings experienced by the more conventional lovers in sixteenth-century poetry (sighs, fevers, tears)

a forward spring remove: postpone an early spring

the plaguie Bill: the weekly list of deaths from the plague in London

which quarrels move: who provoke quarrels

Call her one . . . owne cost die: in their mutual obsession they resemble the moths burned up in the candle flame they circle around, and the candles which gradually melt away. 'Die' was a colloquial term for orgasm, and it may that Donne refers here to a somewhat depressing contemporary theory that each act of love-making reduces the length of life by a full day

the'Eagle and the Dove: symbols of strength and gentleness, and also of aggression and submissiveness. The lovers unite qualities usually held to be opposites, or, developing the thought of the previous lines, they are each other's victims and oppressors

The Phoenix ridle: the phoenix was a mythical bird. It was a riddle how it perpetuated its species, since there was never more than one bird at any time; it was believed to consume itself periodically in fire, and to rise renewed but unchanged from its own ashes

hath more wit/By us: makes better sense because of us, is explained by us

one neutrall thing: in the act of love-making they combine male and female, and so are, like the bird, sexually neutral

dye and rise the same: see note on 'Call her one . . . ' above. Their love is unchanging before, during and after love-making

prove/Mysterious: become a mystery. Their unchanging passion puts them, like the phoenix or like the truths of religion, beyond the grasp of reason

unfit: improper, unsuitable

if no peece of Chronicle wee prove: even if our story will not be found in the history books

sonnets: love lyrics

well wrought: beautifully made (like a lyric)

becomes: suits, is appropriate to

approve: acknowledge

***Canoniz'd*:** made into saints. In Roman Catholic doctrine, men ask the saints to pray for them

invoke us: call on us, pray to us

one anothers hermitage: provided a spiritual refuge for each other

You, . . . that now is rage: later lovers, who experience love only as a raging frustration, will recognise from the love lyrics that for Donne and his mistress it was a condition of fulfilled peace

Who did the whole worlds soule extract . . . Courts: two main metaphors are behind these highly compressed lines, as well as a punning shift in the meaning of 'glasses'. An alchemist extracts the essential quality of a substance by driving it through his apparatus into glass vessels or containers (the first metaphor); their passionate relationship has enabled them to extract the soul of the whole world, which is now held in the looking-glasses or mirrors of their eyes (the pun). What is actually reflected in their eyes is the image of the other, but as each is the whole world to the other (the second metaphor), this image epitomises, or represents in miniature form, the outer world of countries, towns and courts. Their eyes see and reflect, hence the reference to both 'mirrors' and 'spies'

Beg from above/A patterne of your love!: ask heaven to grant us the blessing of a love like yours. The word 'love' is the chief rhyming word throughout the poem, used at the end of the first and last lines of each stanza

'Song: Sweetest love, I do not goe'

This is a simple but eloquent poem on the theme of parting, and another of the poems said in some manuscripts to have been written to fit an existing tune.

NOTES AND GLOSSARY:

'tis best/ . . . fain'd deaths to dye: to prepare myself for my real death by these simulated deaths of parting from you. The idea that separation is a kind of death is frequent in Donne's writing

sense: feeling

come bad chance . . . to'advance: if misfortune comes we feed it by our own misery, and so allow it to gain a more complete and lasting hold on us

sigh'st my soule away: in both Greek and Latin (both of which Donne knew) the same word is used for both 'breath' and 'soul'

unkindly kinde: her grief reveals her love, but it nonetheless causes him harm

in thine my life thou waste: in weakening herself in grief she weakens him as well

divining: prophetic

Forethinke: foresee, imagine. Compare 'Elegie: On his Mistris', ll.55–6, for the general thought

'Aire and Angels'

This is one of the most difficult of the *Songs and Sonnets*, but it is also one of the finest, and deserves a rather fuller introductory note to set out the main lines of the poem's argument. Points of difficulty are discussed in the detailed notes which follow.

The starting point of the poem is the poet's sense that *he loves*, that is, he is aware that something has called his love into existence. But what does it mean to speak of 'my love'? This is the question to be answered in the poem.

The first six lines consider the idea that was put forward by some Italian theorists of love in the sixteenth century: that lovers in fact fall in love not with this or that individual person, but with a divine radiance which may be glimpsed shining through the human body (see the notes to ll.1–2 below for fuller comment on these ideas). This notion of a love which would be entirely spiritual is dismissed with laughter: such a love would be 'lovely' and 'glorious', but it would be the love of 'nothing'.

Donne continues by granting that love comes from the soul; but just as his soul needed to inhabit his body before it could become real and active in this world (otherwise it could 'nothing doe'), so his love too must take on a body. This leads him to the second suggested answer to his question: that to speak of 'my love' is in fact to speak of the woman who is physically present before him. At first he accepts this as an answer ('I allow'). But her physical presence does not so much keep his love steady (as 'ballast' keeps a boat steady), as bewilder and overwhelm him with so much beauty: she is 'Extreme, and scatt'ring bright', perhaps the loveliest compliment ever paid in English poetry.

Neither of these two answers has proved satisfactory. Love is not simply a quality of the spirit, nor simply a quality of the body (it does not 'inhere' in either). But his love is real, and it does have an existence. For a final answer to his question he puts to new use an idea he had touched on earlier. An angel belongs to the realm of spirit, but to be known and recognised in this world it needs to inhabit some sort of body. This parallels the situation of his love. An angel, according to one medieval theory, takes on a body of air, which is the material element nearest to it in character; his love will adopt for its body the element of her love for him. (Donne uses the word 'sphere', on which see the note below.) This answer to Donne's question is not unlike the one arrived at in a very different mood in 'Loves Deity':

> It cannot bee
> Love, till I love her, that loves me.

It is her love for him that gives reality and existence to his love for her. The earliest opposition of spiritual and physical has been swept aside as misleading, and, in the last analysis, irrelevant.

NOTES AND GLOSSARY:

Twice or thrice ... thy face or name: some Christian thinkers in sixteenth-century Italy held that the true beauty of the body is only an outward sign of the moral and spiritual beauty of the soul, which itself radiates outwards from the absolute truth and beauty of God himself. Accordingly, they also held that the love of any beautiful woman was only a step towards love of the spiritual beauty she shared with all other beautiful women, and that in turn was only a step towards love of the Heavenly Beauty of God. In loving other women in the past, then, Donne was loving an idea which is more fully revealed in her. See 'The Good-Morrow', ll.6–7

So in a voice ... and worship'd bee: an angel which appears to man in the form of a voice or a flickering flame is only imperfectly revealed, just as the idea of an absolute beauty is only imperfectly revealed in the forms of individual women

still: always

thou: the idea revealed through her

limmes: limbs

subtile: ethereal, intangible
assume: put on
wares: usually, the goods that might be carried on board a ship; here, her physical beauties, which 'sink' or overwhelm him
overfraught: overloaded
Ev'ry thy haire: each single hair
some fitter must be sought: some more suitable body for his love to take on
inhere: exist in, abide permanently in
aire, not pure as it, yet pure: an angel is a spirit, and therefore more pure than any material element, but air is also 'pure' in the sense that it is unmixed (and so not able to decay: see notes to 'The Good-Morrow', l.19, 'What ever dyes . . . ')
spheare: the main sense of the word here is 'element'. But Donne also has in mind a second idea: each planet and star was believed to consist of a hollow sphere within which was a controlling Intelligence, that is, an angel. Her love is thus like a hollow sphere which encloses and holds his love, and his love is like the angel which guides and directs a star
Just such disparitie . . . will ever bee: there is a disparity, or inequality, between the love of a man and the love of a woman, just as there is between the purity of an angel and the lesser purity of the air from which it forms its visible body. These lines have caused much difficulty, since they seem to belittle women in general at the close of a poem which has at its centre a love and reverence for the one woman addressed. The lines have been interpreted as a poor joke; as the expression of a commonplace idea of Donne's time; and as a way of filling out a complex stanza form after the poet had run out of ideas. None of these explanations is satisfactory. The solution seems to be that Donne does not like to close a poem on an intense note, but prefers to withdraw a little, as if to allow the woman time to absorb and respond to what has been said. In this case the poem returns to the gentle but slightly teasing tone of the opening lines. For a poem with a similar pattern, compare 'Loves Growth'

'The Anniversarie'

In this poem Donne meditates on the timelessness of the world of love, set against the world of time in which all human love necessarily takes place, and which is of course implied by the very idea of a poem celebrating the anniversary of their first meeting. This is perhaps one of the finest short poems in the language.

NOTES AND GLOSSARY:

as they passe: probably referring to the Kings and their favourites, and to 'times'; the sun makes time, even as time, and all those subject to time, pass

his: its

Two graves: presumably they are not man and wife, and so will not be allowed to share a grave

dwells: lives permanently

inmates: temporary lodgers

prove/This, or a love increased there above: experience this same, or perhaps an even greater love, in heaven

soules from their graves remove: the body is seen as the grave of the soul, and death as the soul's release

throughly: thoroughly, completely

wee no more, than all the rest: in heaven all are fully blessed according to their capacity, so there can be no place for the sense of exceptional happiness they feel here in this world

nor of such subjects bee: nor can be subjects of such Kings as themselves

refraine: hold back, keep under control

love nobly: their nobility will consist in their not being disturbed by either genuine or imaginary fears

till we attaine/To write threescore: till we reach the sixtieth anniversary of our love

'Twicknam Garden'

This poem is Donne's variation on a standard poetic theme, the contrast between the joys of spring and the miseries of the lover whose lady is unkind. Lucy, Countess of Bedford, lived at Twickenham (not far from London) from 1608 to 1617, during which time she was the patroness of Donne as well as of other poets.

NOTES AND GLOSSARY:

Blasted with sighs: withered by the bitter air of his own sighs

surrounded: flooded

balmes: healing influences
else: apart from his misery
selfe traytor: one who betrays or harms himself
spider love: spiders were popularly supposed to be full of poison
transubstantiates all: transforms everything into another substance
Manna to gall: that which should be sweet and nourishing is turned into something bitter and hurtful
the serpent: alluding to the Old Testament story in which the devil, disguised as a serpent, tempted Eve to desire that which was forbidden (see Genesis 3)
'twere wholesomer for mee: it would be better for me
grave: heavy, severe
Love let mee/ . . . of this place bee: if he could be transformed into some unfeeling vegetable or statue, he could remain in the garden without being conscious of his own pain, or of its beauty which seems to mock his feelings of misery
mandrake: the mandrake plant was supposed to groan if uprooted (some manuscripts read 'groan' rather than 'grow')
Who's therefore true . . . kills me: she is unique among women in being faithful, but her fidelity (to someone else) is killing him with grief

'Loves Growth'

In the first stanza Donne argues that love is not 'pure' but 'mixt', a compound of both sexual and spiritual feelings. The idea is stated in this summary way in l.14. But in the second stanza the tone deepens, and the summary gives way to the natural imagery which more profoundly suggests the real unity of the experience.

NOTES AND GLOSSARY:

pure: as usually in Donne, not 'morally upright' but 'simple, unmixed', and therefore incapable of any change or decay
it doth endure/Vicissitude: it does change and fluctuate
which cures all sorrow/With more: alluding to the medical theory that a disease was to be cured by the application of a like medicine
quintessence: the essence of anything after all impurities were removed, thus isolating whatever was valuable and sustaining in it

paining soule, or sense: as love is a compound, it can cause pain to both the body and the soul

working vigour: strength and energy (including sexual energies)

abstract: non-physical

as they use/To say . . . their Muse: as is generally said by those poets who are in love with poetry rather than with a woman. In Greek mythology the nine Muses presided over the various forms of the arts and sciences; Donne is mocking the portrayal of love in conventional Petrarchan poetry

elemented: composed of a variety of elements

do: act (compare 1.19, 'Gentle love deeds')

And yet . . . but showne: the stars are not made larger by the sun, but only made more visible by its light; so too their love will not be made greater by a new sexual element, but will only become more forcibly real to them (the stars were believed to reflect light from the sun)

If, as in water stir'd . . . such additions take: the suggestion is that the 'love deeds' would develop from their love as naturally and inevitably as the stirring of water produces a series of circles all centred on the first movement

like to many spheares . . . unto thee: their acts of love will all revolve around her, just as the various spheres which make up the heavens revolve around the earth

heate: energy, especially sexual energy

in times of action: in times of war

remit: cancel

abate: put an end to. The poem, which had begun by denying the infinity of love, concludes by asserting it

'The Dream'

In this poem as in 'The Flea' or in 'Twicknam Garden', Donne offers a variation on a standard poetic theme. Here the theme is that of the poet's dream or daydream in which his mistress grants him what she has always refused in the waking world.

NOTES AND GLOSSARY:

It was a theame/ . . . for phantasie: the subject matter of his dream was better suited to waking thought than to sleeping imagination

NOTES AND GLOSSARY:

so true . . . fables histories: she is the essence of truth itself, so that even a thought of her turns dreams or stories into true histories

Tapers light: candlelight

(For thou lov'st truth): he is about to make a confession, and does so because he knows she would wish him to tell the truth

an Angell: the sense becomes clear as the poem continues: at first he thought she was *only* an angel

beyond an Angels art: angels were not believed to be able to read men's thoughts

it could not chuse but bee/Prophane: it would necessarily be profane, or blasphemous

any thing but thee: that is, anything less than herself, as, for example, a mere angel

show'd thee, thee: proved your identity to me

as torches . . . put out: a torch which had been lit briefly, and then extinguished, was easier to re-light than a fresh torch

kindle: set alight

goest to come: go away intending to return later

'A Valediction: of Weeping'

A valedictory poem is one bidding farewell. Here the poem begins with an elaborate defence of the poet's tears at parting, but when the lady too begins to weep (at 1.17), the mood becomes more urgent, and the poet pleads for calm and restraint.

NOTES AND GLOSSARY:

whil'st I stay here: while I am still here

thy face . . . something worth: the tears reflect her likeness, as a coin carries the likeness of a ruler, and this gives them a value

Pregnant: full

emblemes of more: an emblem is a picture with a symbolic content; the tear carrying her likeness breaks on falling to the ground, which he interprets as an image of how they too will be broken to 'nothing' when parted from each other

on a divers shore: in different countries, with the sea between them

make that, which was nothing, *All*: the plain globe is like a nought, or nothing; when the mapped paper is pasted on to it, it represents the world, or all

So doth each teare/ . . . by that impression grow: his blank tears become a world when they carry her image, because she is the world to him

thy teares . . . my heaven dissolved so: as the lady (the poet's heaven) begins to weep she drowns all the little worlds that her image had made of his tears

O more than Moone . . . in thy spheare: 'sphere' refers both to the range of power of a heavenly body (which would now be described as its gravitational field), and to her power over him. The moon has power over the tides, but she is more powerful, in that she draws forth seas of tears which destroy worlds

in thine armes: the place above all others where he should be safe

forbeare/To teach: do not teach

Since thou and I . . . the others death: see the note on 'sigh'st my soule away', in 'Song: Sweetest love, I do not goe', l.26

'Loves Alchymie'

This is the most savage of all the poems in which Donne denounces love. The title is explained by the final two lines: the lover is like a deluded alchemist who has sought in love the elixir which will cure all diseases and even prolong life, but he will have in the end to be content with whatever benefit is to be found in sexually entering a dead lump of mindless flesh; because that is the most one can expect of a woman.

NOTES AND GLOSSARY:

centrique: central. There is a direct sexual reference in these first two lines

told: counted

'tis imposture all: it is all a cheat; love has no hidden mystery

as no chymique . . . or med'cinall: just as no alchemist ever found the elixir which would cure all diseases and prolong life, but was nonetheless delighted and encouraged if by chance he discovered something which smelled sweet, or had some medicinal value

a winter-seeming summers night: love is as brief as a summer night, but as bleak and barren as a winter one

our day: our time of healthy life. See note to 'The Canonization', l.21

my man: my servant. The suggestion is that love is a commonplace affair, and not a high spiritual state to be attained only by a refined few

the short scorne of a Bridegroomes play: the brief humiliation of the role of a bridegroom

Which he in her Angelique findes: it is her mind which he finds angelic

that dayes rude hoarse minstralsey: the crude and disagreeable music used at the wedding festivities

the spheares: the harmonious movements of the various heavenly bodies were believed to produce a music too perfect to be heard by ordinary human ears

at their best/Sweetnesse and wit: at their loveliest and cleverest

Mummy: lumps of dead flesh. Dead bodies were sometimes preserved in bitumen for the sake of their supposed medicinal value

possest: there are two meanings here: (*a*) sexually possessed; (*b*) inhabited by a demon or evil spirit, which gives the appearance of life to the 'Mummy'. The suggestion is that there may be some medicinal value in entering a woman's body, but not because of any meeting of the minds: all that is to be met there is the evil spirit which animates the body

'A Nocturnall upon S. Lucies Day'

There is some controversy as to the identity of the person to whom this poem refers. Whatever the background to the poem, it is a sombre and profoundly moving meditation on the sense of absolute loss.

NOTES AND GLOSSARY:

S. Lucies day: St Lucy's day, 13 December, was traditionally regarded as the Winter Solstice, or shortest day

spent: exhausted

flasks: the stars, which were supposed to store up energy from the sun, as flasks (cases of metal or horn) were used to store gunpowder

light squibs: weak flashes

the generall balme: sixteenth-century medical theory held that death and decay followed the using up of the 'balm' or life-giving natural essence contained in all living bodies

hydroptique: suffering from dropsy and therefore afflicted with a raging thirst. All the life-giving forces in nature have been swallowed up by the diseased earth

Whither . . . life in shrunke: life has shrunk down into the earth during the winter, as a dying man may be supposed to shrink down to the foot of the bed

enterr'd: buried

epitaph: memorial inscription on a gravestone. His condition of grief is like a brief history or memorial of the general condition of lifelessness

In whom love wrought . . . nothingnesse: his love has extracted the very essence of nothingness, instead of the elixir of life usually sought by the alchemist

dull privations: privation refers to the absence of something; dull privations would be those frustrations or disappointments which leave one feeling heavy and lifeless

ruin'd: destroyed

re-begot: re-born

All others, . . . whence they beeing have: human life ('beeing') depends on and is fed by the life-giving forces present throughout all created nature. Donne alone is excluded from this source of being

limbecke: alembic

Oft a flood . . . us two: compare 'A Valediction: of Weeping', ll.14–18, and the notes to those lines

oft did we grow . . . /Care to ought else: the world was supposed to have been created out of chaos. Whenever they showed concern for anything except each other the world of their love collapsed back into the condition of chaos

absences/ . . . made us carcasses: physical separations in which however their souls remained united, so that their bodies were left as lifeless shells

Of the first nothing, the Elixer grown: he has become not only the essence of nothing, but the essence of that first, original nothing which existed before the world began

I should preferre/ . . . some means: even a beast is capable of making choices; he no longer is able to do so

Yea plants, yea stones detest: in a sermon Donne considers the possibility that even the stones may have life

All, all some properties invest: every created thing has some characteristics

If I an ordinary nothing . . . be here: an ordinary nothing is merely the absence of something, and thus, like the shadow, implies the existence or at least the possible existence of something. He however is 'None', an absolute nothing

my Sunne: his lady

The Goat: the sun enters the sign of the Goat (Capricorn) at the Winter Solstice, before the days begin to lengthen again
new lust: the goat was considred the most lustful of animals. As the season changes to spring, all other lovers will feel their energies and desires restored
long nights festivall: long sleep of death. There is a slight suggestion in the phrase of her eventual resurrection
Let mee prepare towards her: dedicate himself to her, contemplate the fact of her death, rather than the eventual return of the summer
Vigill: to keep vigil is to sit up at night beside a dead body
Eve: the evening before a saint's day or other church festival

'The Apparition'

Donne here demonstrates his individuality by bringing together two conventional themes: the rejected lover's complaint that his lady's chastity is killing him, and the warning that in old age she will long in vain for the pleasure she now refuses to grant him.

NOTES AND GLOSSARY:
solicitation: entreaty, pleading
fain'd vestall: the lady has falsely claimed to be dedicated to preserving her virginity (priestesses at the Roman temple of Vesta swore an oath of virginity)
winke: flicker, as if about to go out
whose thou art then: the lover who will possess you at that time
Aspen: trembling, as the tree of the same name does in even a slight breeze
quicksilver: mercury. This metal has a semi-liquid form, and in small quantities could resemble beads of sweat
A veryer ghost than I: even more a ghost than I shall be
What I will say . . . still innocent: if he makes her so afraid with his threats that she decides to remain chaste after his death, he will not have the satisfaction of seeing her suffer in the way that he predicts
spent: his love is finished. But the whole basis of the poem, despite this moment of defiance, is his continuing but hopeless love for her

'A Valediction: forbidding mourning'

In his *Life of Dr John Donne*, Izaac Walton says that Donne gave this poem to his wife before leaving to travel in France, Germany and Belgium in 1611. Modern editors have been inclined to doubt this claim, which was not made until the fourth edition of Walton's work (first edition 1640; fourth edition 1675).

NOTES AND GLOSSARY:

teare-floods . . . sigh-tempests: the conventional expressions of grief

move: cause

'Twere prophanation . . . the layetie our love: see the note on 'prophane men', 'The Undertaking' (l.22)

Moving of th'earth . . . is innocent: the contrast is between obvious occasional movements of the earth, such as earthquakes, which leave men counting the cost of the damage done and anxious about what possibly worse disaster such an event may foreshadow, and the continual trembling movement which was believed to run through the whole universe, but which nonetheless passed unnoticed, neither causing nor foretelling any harm. It is of course to this second kind of movement that the movements of feeling in the lovers are likened

sublunary: changeable

(Whose soule is sense): the essence of whose love is physical

admit: allow

elemented it: composed it. The essentially physical love cannot survive physical separation

so much refin'd/ . . . what it is: a favourite idea in Donne's poetry. Their love has reached that high level at which it becomes a mystery of which even they themselves cannot give an account. Compare 'The Extasie', ll.21–2

inter-assured: mutually confident

endure not yet/A breach: nonetheless do not suffer a break

gold to ayery thinnesse beate: gold is beaten out to make gold leaf

compasses: instrument used for drawing circles

as it comes home: as the two legs of the compass are closed after use

firmnes: the physical stiffness of the leg of the compass; the moral strength he is urging on her throughout the poem

makes my circle just: makes me complete a perfect circle; gives a point and direction to my journey

makes me end, where I begunne: logically the compass analogy breaks down here. The lady is now thought of as both the point on the circumference of the circle where he started, and to which he returns in completing the circle, and as the centre, the still point around which he revolves. This is not so much a slip as a sign of the pressure of feeling in the poem

'The Exstasie'

This has been one of the most discussed of Donne's poems. It may be divided into three sections. The first (ll.1–20) describes the situation, in which the souls of the two lovers go out from their bodies (this is the literal meaning of 'ecstasy'). The second section (ll.21–48) employs the device of an imaginary listener and observer, in order to summarise what is communicated by the two souls. The last part of the poem puts forward reasons for the souls to return to their bodies: among these are the desirability of sexual love, and the duty to 'reveal' love to those who would be too 'weak' to believe in love without some such sign.

NOTES AND GLOSSARY:

The violets: the violet was traditionally associated with faithful love

fast balme: the warm moisture that holds them fast together

Our eye-beames twisted: one theory of sight held that it was caused by the contact of a beam sent out from the eye with the object seen. Their eye-beams are twisted because they are looking at each other

to'entergraft: a gardener produces a graft by inserting a shoot into a slit made in another plant, so that the sap can circulate through both freely. Their fingers are twined together, as if the same 'balm' flowed through both of them

to get: to beget, to create

As 'twixt two equall Armies . . . her, and mee: the uncertain outcome of a battle was sometimes represented by artists by a pair of scales hung ('suspended') between the two armies. Here the bodies are like the opposed armies; the souls are sent out, like envoys, to 'negotiate' between them

sepulchrall statues: statues on tombs

a new concoction: the process of refining metals and minerals by heat. The observer will be even more 'refined' after he has heard them

unperplex: resolve their difficulties

Wee see, we saw not what did move: in their state of ecstasy, or separation from their bodies, they realise that they had not previously understood what attracted them to each other

Mixture of things, they know not what: the soul was presumed to be a mixture of things because it had to perform many different functions. It was a common idea that we are unaware of the nature of our own souls

Love . . . doth mixe againe: love further mixes these souls, which are already a mixture of things

both one, each this and that: see 'The Good-Morow', note to l.14 ('Let us possess . . . '), for this idea of one person made out of two

When love . . . two soules: when love so combines two separate souls that they become one new soul. Compare 'entergraft' in l.9

Defects of lonelinesse controules: the two souls united together are stronger than either was separately, because each can remedy the weaknesses or 'defects' of the other

atomies: atoms

soules, whom no change can invade: the soul, unlike the body, was not obliged to suffer change. Their ecstasy has shown them that their love exists on the level of the soul rather than on the level of the body, and consequently their love too is free from change. See 'A Valediction: forbidding mourning', ll.13–16, and the notes on these lines

forbeare: avoid, keep away from

Wee are/Th'intelligences, they the spheare: they are related to their bodies just as an angel is related to the sphere it controls. See 'Aire and Angels', l.25 and note

Yeelded their forces, sense, to us: the natural forces of the body are the powers of the senses. They have been able to achieve their state of ecstasy because their bodies temporarily gave up these powers

Nor are drosse to us: in some accounts of love, the body was seen as impure matter to be left behind or discarded. Donne here, as usually, rejects this view

allay: alloy, that is, a base metal mixed in with one of a higher value. Donne's distinction between dross and alloy is a slight one: the body is not to be rejected, but it is the inferior element in the body – soul partnership. The line is not very satisfactory

On man heavens influence . . . to body first repaire: the planets and stars can only influence man by first affecting the air. Sometimes, therefore, a spiritual force requires a physical medium through which to work. In the same way, the spiritual union of their souls may require the physical union of their bodies

repaire: goes to

As our blood labours . . . which makes us man: since man was composed of the two dissimilar components, body and soul, it was held that there must be a link connecting the two; this link was the vapour, or spirit, produced by the blood

need: are needed

subtile: two meanings here: (*a*) ethereal, impalpable; (*b*) complex. Compare modern usages of the word 'fine'

affections: passions

faculties: powers of action

That sense may reach and apprehend: that are within the range of the senses

Else a great Prince in prison lies: the loving self is only made free if body and soul work together in the harmony described in ll.61–7

that so/Weake men . . . the body is his booke: see the note introducing this poem, and 'Elegie: To his Mistris going to Bed', ll.40–3, and notes

dialogue of one: see l.26 of the poem

Let his still mark us, . . . to bodies gone: he will realise how little their love is altered by the return of their souls to their bodies. Until this point, the bystander has been listening; the change to a bystander who watches the couple making love provides an unsatisfactory close to the poem

'Loves Deitie'

A rather formal poem, based on the idea of a 'golden age' in which love was given and accepted freely. Donne characteristically complicates the poem in the last verse.

NOTES AND GLOSSARY:

before the god of love was borne: that is, in the days when love could be offered and enjoyed in total freedom

hee, who then lov'd most: even the greatest lover of those days
produc'd a destinee: appointed a special fate for lovers
that vice-nature, custome, lets it be: as we grow accustomed to our destiny, and it becomes second nature to us, we no longer try to resist it
meant not so much: did not intend love to have so much authority and power
even: equal
His office . . . /Actives to passives: it was his task obligingly to pair up men and women (those who make the advances, and those who accept them)
Correspondencie/Only his subject was: his only business was to ensure a perfect and equal match
prerogative: right of authority
Jove: Jupiter, the greatest of the ancient Roman gods
To rage . . . God of Love: the God of Love now claims new rights, and dictates the feelings and actions of unhappy and frustrated lovers as well
ungod: rebel against, overthrow
child: Cupid, the God of Love, is usually represented as a winged child armed with a bow and arrows
murmure: complain
loves before: already has a lover
Falshood is worse . . . should love mee: she would have to be false to her present lover in order to love the poet; rather than see her turn false, he would prefer that she continue to hate him

'The Will'

This is another rather formal poem. The lady to whom he offered his love did not value it as he thought she ought to; therefore he proposes to leave all his qualities and possessions to those who are least likely to value them properly. The poem thus makes a number of satirical hits, usually at rather obvious targets, but the tone of the poem also implies a satirical view of the poet himself.

NOTES AND GLOSSARY:
Argus: in Greek mythology, a giant with a hundred eyes
If they be blinde: the God of Love is often represented blindfolded
Fame: rumour, gossip
who'had twenty more: twenty more lovers
the planets: planets were sometimes known as wandering stars, and so were supposed incapable of constancy

ingenuity: ingenuousness, frankness

Jesuites: members of the Roman Catholic Society of Jesus, an extremely active Catholic group which had been founded by Ignatius Loyola (1491–1556) in 1534. The common complaint against the Jesuits in Donne's day was their defence of equivocation, the use of ambiguous words so as to conceal a true meaning

Buffones: fools, clowns

My silence . . . hath beene: a stock joke against travellers who told improbable tales of things seen and done on their voyages

Capuchin: member of a monastic order vowed to absolute poverty

My faith . . . /Of Amsterdam: Roman Catholic teaching argued that salvation depended on good works as well as faith. The Schismatics were their logical opposites, an extreme Puritan group who believed that salvation depended on faith alone

Courtship: civility, courtliness of manner. The implication is that scholars are generally lacking in any elegance of manners

bare: naked

gamesters: gamblers

that holds my love disparity: who considers his love beneath her dignity, not worth having

Mine industrie to foes: he owes his hard work to the opponents against whom he had to defend himself

Schoolmen: medieval theologians, whose endlessly subtle arguments led to doubt and uncertainty

excesse: sickness was supposed to result from the excess of some element in the constitution

my wit: his cleverness

the passing bell: the church bell rung to announce someone's death

physick bookes: medical books

writen rowles/Of Morall counsels: documents full of good advice

Bedlam: the London lunatic asylum

My brazen medals: ancient bronze coins, no longer in use as currency, and so useless to the starving

dost my gifts thus disproportion: she claims to have no use for the things he is able to offer her

undoe: ruin, defeat

all your beauties will bee no more worth: her beauty is only precious so long as she has someone to admire it

who doth neglect both mee and thee: it is hard to see how a lady with twenty lovers (l.8) can be accused of neglecting the God of Love. Perhaps she has refused all the others as well, or perhaps he feels his love is the only true one; lovers, especially poetic lovers, are inclined to be egotistic

practise: put into practice

all three: poet, lady, and Love himself

'The Relique'

The poet argues that the true miracle of his love for the lady of the poem, even though it may never be understood, is that it is a love not based on sexual desire.

NOTES AND GLOSSARY:

Relique: a relic is a part of the body or belongings of a holy person, kept after his or her death as an object of worship or reverence. The reverencing of relics had been abandoned by the Reformed churches in Donne's day

When my grave . . . entertaine: this practice was not uncommon until quite recent times

that woman-head: that womanly nature. The sexual reference of these lines is re-inforced by the similarity of 'woman-head' to 'maidenhead'

device: trick. At the Day of Resurrection (the 'last busie day') our souls will have to travel the earth to gather our scattered bodily members. The trick therefore is to put a part of each lover in the same grave, so that they will be able to meet again briefly even on the very last day

fall: happen

Where mis-devotion doth command: where false worship, as of relics, is still practised

a Mary Magdalen: the bright hair round his wrist will suggest St Mary Magdalen to the grave-digger, because she was always represented in art with long golden hair (she was identified with the 'sinner' who washed Christ's feet with her hair: see the Bible, Luke 7)

A something else: probably a dismissive phrase: he will be supposed one of her lovers, to whom she gave the hair as a token before her reform

thereby: by the decision of the King and the Bishop

at such times: at such periods of mistaken belief

knew not what wee lov'd, nor why: compare 'A Valediction: forbidding mourning', ll.17–18

Difference of sex . . . Angells doe: similar to angels who have no sexual nature, their love had no sexual element

meales: the kiss is seen as the food of the soul

the seales/ . . . sets free: the restrictions on human love-making, which do not belong to Nature, but are the consequences of relatively recent man-made laws and conventions. The word 'injur'd' suggests that the poet is not completely convinced that the absence of any sexual element in their love is an unmixed good; it may be suggested that the sexual knowingness of ll.3–4 is not quite consistent with a whole-hearted celebration of entirely spiritual love

These miracles wee did: i.e., not the miracles that an age of mis-devotion will attribute to them, but the nonetheless genuine miracle of an exceptional love

'The Expiration'

This poem is based on an idea which also appears in 'Song (Sweetest love, I do not goe)', that the soul is in the breath, and on the thought to which Donne returns often, that parting resembles death.

NOTES AND GLOSSARY:

vapors: causes to evaporate

benight: turn into night

We ask'd none leave . . . as saying, Goe: they did not ask anyone for permission to love, nor will they allow anyone the power to destroy them simply by ordering them to part

Except: unless

going, and bidding goe: leaving her, and telling her to leave him

From the *Divine Poems*

Most of Donne's *Divine Poems* come from the middle period of his life, and the strain of those years of disappointment, ill-health and financial insecurity is often evident. These are not poems celebrating moments of vision in which the poet had glimpsed his ultimate union with God or felt a renewed assurance of the promise of heavenly bliss; rather, they are poems marked by an effort of the will, in which Donne sought to examine and discipline his mind, and in many of them the freedom and vitality so characteristic of the love poetry are replaced by a mood which borders on despair. Even some of the most famous of the *Divine Poems* have about them something forced and unnatural; the sonnet 'Batter my heart', for example, contrives to be at one and the same time a lavish and wilful display of Donne's intellectual virtuosity, and an assertion of the poet's desire to surrender his individuality by submitting entirely to the will of God. At least two of the *Divine Poems*, however, the sonnet 'Since she whome I lovd' and the late 'A Hymne to God the Father', equal the achievement of even the finest of the *Songs and Sonnets*, and deserve to hold a place of honour among English religious poems.

HOLY SONNETS: DIVINE MEDITATIONS

The meditation is a form of religious exercise in which memory and imagination are used systematically to help focus and encourage a mood of devotion: for example, a meditation on the theme of God's love towards man might begin with an attempt to imagine the sufferings of Christ on the Cross, while a meditation on the theme of God's eventual judgement on mankind might begin with an attempt to imagine the fears a man might feel during the night before his death. Meditation was widely practised throughout the sixteenth and seventeenth centuries, but it was especially favoured by the Jesuits, and it is likely that Donne was introduced to the practice by his early teachers (the *Spiritual Exercises* of Ignatius Loyola received papal approval in 1548). In this sequence of six sonnets, Donne meditates on two related themes: personal sinfulness, and the judgement of God on sinners.

'As due by many titles'

The argument of the poem is that Donne belongs to God by right; but in his despair he feels that God has abandoned him, and only the Devil seeks him.

NOTES AND GLOSSARY:

titles: legal rights

resigne: surrender

decay'd: corrupted by sin

blood: see note on 'whose paines . . . repaid' below

thy sonne . . . to shine: playing upon 'son' and 'sun'. The believing Christian is 'the child of God'; according to the biblical promise, the 'righteous' will 'shine forth' like the 'sun' at the end of the world (see Matthew 13:43)

whose paines . . . repaid: Christ's sufferings on the Cross were seen as the payment of a ransom, freeing those who held to the Christian faith from the pains they would otherwise have had to endure in hell

Thy sheepe: God's love for mankind is often compared in the Bible to that of the shepherd for his sheep
thine image: in the biblical account, 'God created man in his own image' (see Genesis 1:27)
a temple of thy Spirit divine: according to Christian teaching, the Holy Spirit dwells in all Christian believers, who may thus be said to resemble temples
usurpe in mee: unjustly claim possession of me (compare the first line of the poem)
that's thy right: that which rightly belongs to God
Except: unless

'Oh my blacke Soule!'

This poem is a prayer for the grace without which the poet cannot be truly repentant of his sins.

NOTES AND GLOSSARY:
summoned/By sicknesse . . . champion: the reference is to a joust or tournament, where the herald summoned two rivals to combat; a champion was one who fought for or on behalf of someone else
durst not turne: does not dare to return
deaths doome: the sentence of death
damn'd: condemned
hal'd: dragged
Yet grace . . . grace to beginne: in line 9 'grace' is the mercy of God, which would not be denied to those who truly repented; in line 10 it refers to the state of mind in which the need for repentance is admitted, and which could only come about as the result of God's prompting
might: power, property
white: white was the colour of innocence

'This is my playes last scene'

In this poem Donne imagines that he is on his death-bed preparing to meet God's judgement. It is useful to compare this poem with the preparations Donne did in fact make for his death in 1631 (see Part 1 of these Notes).

NOTES AND GLOSSARY:
My spans last inch: a span is a small distance, or brief length of time
unjoynt: separate

I shall sleepe . . . my ever-waking part: in these lines 'I' is the body, the 'ever-waking part' the soul. Donne believed that the soul was judged at the very instant of death, while the resurrection of the body had to wait until the final Day of Judgement (compare the general thought of 'The Relique', ll.8–11)

that all may have their right: his soul will go to its proper home in heaven, and his body will return to the earth (according to biblical teaching, God made the first man from the dust); it is, therefore, only fitting that his sins should go to their natural home in hell

and would presse me: his sins want to thrust him into hell

Impute me righteous: see the note on 'imputed grace' in 'To his Mistris Going to Bed', l.42

'At the round earths imagin'd corners'

In this poem Donne imagines the Day of Judgement, and begs for time to be allowed for him to repent his sins.

NOTES AND GLOSSARY:

the round earths imagin'd corners: the idea of the 'four corners of the earth' comes from the Bible (see Revelation 7:1)

scattred bodies: the parts of the body scattered over the earth as dust and bones (see note on 'I shall sleepe . . . ' in 'This is my playes last scene', ll.6–7)

flood . . . fire: according to the biblical stories, God had destroyed the world by flood in the time of Noah, and would finally destroy it by, among other things, fire (see Genesis 6–9, and Revelation 6 *et seq*.)

never tast deaths woe: Christ had promised that some of those who heard him speak would never 'taste of death' (see Matthew 16:28)

But let them sleepe: that is, delay the Day of Judgement

'Tis late: it will be too late

Teach mee how to repent: see 'Oh my blacke Soule!', ll.9–10

seal'd my pardon: Christ's death on the Cross purchased an offer of pardon for all men; if Donne learns how to repent his sins, his particular pardon will be confirmed or authorised

'If Poysonous Mineralls'

The poem is a prayer that God will forget the poet's sins, and so allow him to escape the damnation he has deserved.

NOTES AND GLOSSARY:

if that tree . . . else immortall us: death came into the world when Adam and Eve ate the fruit of the tree of the knowledge of good and evil, which God had forbidden (see Genesis 3)

Cannot be damn'd: only creatures capable of a reasoned choice were liable to damnation

And mercy . . . why threatens hee?: why does God angrily threaten eternal punishment when it is easy for him to show mercy, and when to do so increases his glory?

thine onely worthy blood: only the blood of Christ is able to drown the memory of the poet's sins

Lethean flood: in ancient mythology the souls of the dead drank from the river Lethe, whose water had the power of drowning all memory of an earlier existence on earth

That thou remember . . . if thou wilt forget: some people ask God to remember and forgive their sins in terms of a claim on his mercy, since their pardon had been bought by the death of Christ. The poet prefers to hope that God will simply forget his sins (see Jeremiah 31:34)

'Death be not proud'

The argument of the poem is that Death is not all-powerful, since it must eventually give way to eternal life. This is one of the most admired of the Holy Sonnets.

NOTES AND GLOSSARY:

From rest and sleepe . . . much more must flow: since so much pleasure results from rest and sleep, which are only as pictures of death, even more pleasure must result from death itself

Rest . . . deliverie: death provides a rest for man's body, and a birth or liberation for his soul

poppie: the juice of the poppy is a narcotic

And better than thy stroake: the sleep brought on by drugs is heavier and more refreshing than that of death. The idea evidently conflicts with ll.5–6 above

why swell'st thou then?: why do you swell up with pride?
Death thou shalt die: the idea of Death as an enemy to be destroyed comes from the Bible (see I Corinthians 15:26, 54–5)

'Holy Sonnet: Batter my heart'

The plea for God to enter and take over the poet is made through two images of assault, one military and one sexual. The literalness with which both are developed is undoubtedly dramatic, but perhaps leaves the modern reader feeling uncomfortable. See also the note above, introducing the *Divine Poems*.

NOTES AND GLOSSARY:
three-person'd God: the Holy Trinity (God the Father, God the Son, and God the Holy Spirit)
shine: polish
bend: direct, apply
to'another due: owing duty and obedience to another (see 'As due by many titles', ll. 1–2, and note to those lines)
to no end: unsuccessfully
Reason your viceroy . . . should defend: his reason should rule him in God's name and on God's behalf
and would be lov'd faine: the poet wishes to be loved by God
untie, or breake that knot againe: that is, the 'knot' which is said to bind together the partners in a marriage
enthrall mee: make a slave of me
except you ravish mee: unless you rape me

'Holy Sonnet: Since she whome I lovd'

Donne's wife Ann died in August 1617, a few days after giving birth to a still-born child. Throughout the poem Donne tries to persuade himself that her death was in accordance with divine justice and mercy, and to calm his sense of anger and bitterness.

NOTES AND GLOSSARY:
her last debt/To Nature: the idea that we all 'owe' Nature a death was more or less proverbial
and to hers, and my good is dead: the syntax of this line is uncertain. Either (*a*) his wife's death means that she can no longer do anything for her own or for her husband's good; or (*b*) her death has been for her good (she is now in heaven) and for his (since her death he thinks only of heaven). The first reading

offers only the bleak facts, and provides no comfort; the second offers comfort only to a man whose faith is still more powerful than his grief. Possibly both meanings are designedly present in the poem

early: Ann Donne was only thirty-three when she died; the implication of the line is that she died *too* early

ravished: caught up, removed from the earth

in: on

Here: here on earth

whett: encourage

so streames do shew the head: just as a stream can be traced back to *its* source, so all human loves can be traced back to *their* source, which is to be found in the love of God. See 'Aire and Angels', ll. 1–2, and the note to those lines

A holy thirsty dropsy: a reverent but immoderate desire. The sense is that Donne's thirst for God's love has been fed, but he can never feel that it has been fed enough; the thirst is 'holy' because it is not a sin to desire God's love, but it is also diseased (a 'dropsy') because he remains endlessly unsatisfied

when as thou/ . . . offring all thine: God now offers Donne his divine love in exchange for the human love of which he was deprived with the death of his wife

But in thy tender jealousy . . . put thee out: Donne interprets God's treatment of him as that of a jealous and possessive lover. God's jealousy is shown in two ways: firstly, he has removed Donne's wife (his 'saint and Angel'), fearing that Donne might love her too much; and secondly, he has ensured that none of Donne's love would be wasted on the pleasures of this world, by providing for him a life of pain and disappointment

'Good Friday, 1613. Riding Westward'

On Good Friday, 1613, Donne was travelling westwards to visit friends, and it was presumably on this journey that he composed this poem. The argument is in three stages. At first Donne admits that at this time, Good Friday, he should be facing the East, looking towards the place of Christ's death on the Cross (ll.1–14). However, even Nature could not endure the sad spectacle of the dead Christ and the weeping Mary, and for Donne too the sight would be unbearable (ll.15–32). But although he rides away, the image of the Crucifixion is present to his mind; his back is turned only to receive punishment for his sins, and when he has been sufficiently punished, Christ will acknowledge him, and then at last Donne can turn to face Christ.

NOTES AND GLOSSARY:

Let mans Soule . . . devotion is: a man's soul is moved by devotion to God, as a sphere is guided by the Intelligence or angel within it. See 'Aire and Angels', l.25, and note

And as the other Spheares . . . whirld by it: according to sixteenth-century scientists, the natural motion of the spheres which composed the universe was from West to East, but a number of cosmic forces hindered or deflected this movement, including what was known as the *Primum Mobile* or 'first mover'

Hence is't . . . toward the East: his journey carries him physically towards the West, while his devotion compels his soul towards the East

a Sunne . . . endlesse day beget: there is a play here on 'sun' and 'son' (Christ, the Son of God). Christ was raised on the Cross, and endured death ('set'); this sacrifice made eternal life ('endlesse day') available to those who adopted the Christian faith

of too much weight for mee: too great for me to bear

Who sees Gods face . . . must dye: so God told Moses in the Bible (see Exodus 33:20)

that is selfe life: that is the principle of life

Lieutenant: deputy

shrinke: withdraw in horror. Matthew's gospel records the disturbances in nature at the moment of Christ's death (see Matthew 27:51–3)

footstoole: the earth is described as God's footstool in the Bible (see Isaiah 66:1)

the Sunne winke: during the Crucifixion 'there was darkness over all the land' for three hours (see Matthew 27:45)

tune all spheares at once: the movement of all the spheres was believed to produce a perfect musical harmony

Zenith . . . Antipodes: God is the highest point ('endlesse height') both to us and to those on the other side of the world

that blood . . . of all our Soules: the soul was sometimes held to reside, or be seated, in the blood; in fact, Donne argues, all our souls are supported by the blood shed in Christ's self-sacrifice

if not of his: whether or not Christ's soul resided in his blood
Make durt of dust: change dry dust into moist dirt
rag'd: make ragged
Gods partner here: Christ was the child of Mary as well as of God
from mine eye: not present before his eyes
the tree: the Cross
Corrections: punishments which will correct his conduct
Restore thine Image: man was originally made in the image or likeness of God, but this resemblance was destroyed by man's sin. Donne asks to be restored to this original likeness, and so made fit to face Christ

'A Hymne to Christ'

The occasion of this poem was Donne's voyage to Germany in 1619, when he was chaplain to a diplomatic mission; nearing fifty years of age, and in poor spirits, Donne did not expect to return from the journey. The poem is essentially a preparation for death, reminiscent in mood of 'A Nocturnall upon S. Lucies Day'. The image in this poem of God as a demanding and jealous lover, from whom nonetheless Donne seeks still more signs of love, recalls the last eight lines of the sonnet on the death of his wife two years earlier. The fact that 'A Hymne to Christ' is not diminished by comparison with these poems is a measure of its greatness.

NOTES AND GLOSSARY:
thy Arke: the ark, or boat, in which Noah and his family were allowed to escape the flood by which God destroyed the world, was afterwards venerated as a memorial of God's loving care for his chosen people—initially the Jews, subsequently all Christian believers (see Genesis 6–9 for the story)
Which . . . despise: in all the surviving manuscripts of the poem, the last two lines of each stanza appear as one long line (containing seven stresses)
When I have put . . . my sinnes and thee: a prayer for death. Donne is about to travel away from those he loves across the sea and into another country; he wishes also to travel away from his sins across the figurative sea of death into another life in heaven
in my winter: that is, in the later stages of his life
controule: check, limit. Neither Christ nor Christianity would put a check to the love in a soul in a condition of true spiritual harmony

Thou lov'st not . . . thou free/My soule: the demand is that God express his love for the poet by freeing his soul from the love of things or persons in this world, rather than God alone. In order to appreciate fully the severity of this prayer, it is necessary to remember that at this time Donne had seven children to care for

Who ever gives, takes libertie: for the image here, compare 'Batter my heart', ll.9–14, and the notes to those lines

Fame, Wit, Hopes: Donne had pursued these 'false mistresses' right up until his ordination in 1615

To see God only, I goe out of sight: in order to see God and God alone, it is necessary to go where the human power of sight fails: that is, it is necessary to die

And to scape . . . Everlasting night: the close of the poem repeats the prayer for death, in preference to the troubles of this life

'Hymne to God my God, in my sicknesse'

According to Izaac Walton, this poem was written eight days before Donne's death in 1631; another contemporary witness, however, dates it December 1623, when Donne was seriously ill. Like the other *Hymnes*, the poem is a preparation for death, which is welcomed rather than feared.

NOTES AND GLOSSARY:

that Holy roome: heaven

Quire: choir

I tune the instrument: (*a*) he prepares himself for death (so he himself is the instrument); and (*b*) he practises his skill in making hymns to God (so his poetic faculty is the instrument)

Whilst my Physitians . . . I their Mapp: his doctors study him attentively, as geographers study a map

my South-west discoverie: the South is the region of heat, the West the region where the sun declines. Donne interprets his death by fever as the discovery of a route to a new world, i.e., to heaven

***Per fretum febris*:** these Latin words may be translated either (*a*) by the heat of fever, or (*b*) by the narrow passage (straits) of a fever

streights: straits

my West: his death

though theire currants . . . to none: although there is no return from the journey Donne is about to make

As West and East . . . the Resurrection: on a flat map of the world, the extreme West and the extreme East will be the same (as becomes apparent if the map is pasted on a globe); Donne's West (his death) will also be his East (his resurrection, or rebirth in heaven)

Is the Pacifique Sea . . . Is *Jerusalem*?: Donne is thinking of the speculations by medieval geographers as to the location of the Garden of Eden, man's lost Paradise

***Anyan*:** probably Annam, formerly called 'Anian' and placed on the west coast of America, which medieval geographers believed to be separated by only a narrow strait from Asia

All streights . . . are ways to them: the argument is that the straits of '*Anyan*, and *Magellan*, and *Gibraltare*' are the ways to the East, the Pacific, and Jerusalem; however we travel to our eventual home in Paradise, we need to pass through narrow and difficult routes

***Japhet . . . Cham*, or *Sem*:** Japhet, Ham and Shem were the three sons of Noah among whom the world was supposedly divided after the flood

We thinke . . . in one place: it was sometimes held that the Crucifixion took place in what had formerly been the Garden of Eden ('Paradise'). 'Adams tree' is the tree of the knowledge of good and evil, the fruit of which Adam and Eve were forbidden by God

both *Adams*: Christ was seen as a second Adam, especially in the theology of St Paul

the first *Adams* sweat: at the time of the Fall, Adam was told 'in the sweat of thy face shalt thou eat bread' (see Genesis 3:19). Donne is sweating because of the fever

in his purple wrapp'd . . . his other Crowne: the argument is that as Donne undergoes sufferings like those inflicted on Christ at the Crucifixion, so too he may hope to share in the promise of eternal life which Christ won for man by his self-sacrifice. The soldiers who executed Christ clothed him in mockery in a scarlet or purple robe, and a crown of thorns (see Matthew 27:28–9); by 'purple', however, Donne may also be referring to Christ's blood, shed on man's behalf

Therefore . . . the Lord throws down: God is destroying Donne physically in order to raise him to eternal life in heaven

'A Hymne to God the Father'

This is the calmest and most eloquent of the *Hymnes*. It is both a prayer for forgiveness of sin, and a prayer for the conviction that his sins have been forgiven.

NOTES AND GLOSSARY:

that sinne where I begunne/ . . . done before: original sin, that is, the corruption unto which all men are born as a result of the Fall of Adam and Eve

those sinnes . . . doe them still: those sins that he commits every day

thou hast not done: there is a deliberate pun here; (*a*) God has more to do, because there are yet more sins to forgive, and (*b*) God still does not have Donne

that sinne . . . Others to sinne: Donne may not have had anything in particular in mind here; it has been suggested that he is thinking of his abandonment of the Roman Catholic faith, the argument being that Donne, secretly, continued to believe that the Roman Church was the only true Church of God. This reading would also suggest that Donne's entire career in the Church of England was, in effect, encouraging others to sin as he had done

when I have spunne/My last thred: when he comes to the end of his life

the shore: the very border of salvation

thy Sunne/Shall shine: this is one of Donne's favourite puns, on the sun whose warmth is seen as an emblem of God's love for mankind, and on Christ the Son of God who died for mankind

Thou hast done: the pun here resolves the poem; when once God has dealt with the poet's sin of fear, there is no more for God to do, and he will have gained the poet completely

Part 3

Commentary

The *Songs and Sonnets*

For most modern readers the *Songs and Sonnets* represent Donne's most enduring achievement; for many readers they are among the three or four finest collections of love poems in the English language. Yet in all periods there have been distinguished readers unable to accept this high estimate. In the seventeenth century the poet John Dryden (1631–1700) declared that 'Donne perplexes the minds of the fair sex with nice speculations of philosophy, when he should engage their hearts and entertain them with the softness of love'. Samuel Johnson (1709–84), one of the greatest of English critics, voiced similar doubts. In his 'Life of Cowley' (1779) Johnson, borrowing the term from Dryden, described as 'the metaphysical poets' a group of seventeenth-century poets who, whether or not directly influenced by Donne, shared something of his poetic manner and idiom. Johnson alleged that these poets, including Donne, wrote of human life as if they had no share or involvement in it: 'The metaphysical poets were men of learning, and to show their learning was their whole endeavour .... Their courtship was void of fondness, and their lamentation of sorrow ... they never attempted that comprehension and expanse of thought which at once fills the whole mind, and of which the first effect is sudden astonishment, and the second rational admiration.' More recently, the scholar C.S. Lewis has taken this complaint further, and held that 'Donne's love poetry ... largely omits the very thing that all the pother was about': in other words, the *Songs and Sonnets* are a kind of love poetry in which the love is missed out.

These are substantial charges. In effect, the critics quoted here are agreed on three points: firstly, that the difficulties of 'metaphysical poetry', including Donne's, are merely superficial ('to show their learning was their whole endeavour'); secondly, that such poetry is unable adequately to portray human feelings ('their courtship was void of fondness'); and thirdly, that such poetry cannot succeed in engaging the interest of the reader at the deepest levels ('that comprehension and expanse of thought which at once fills the whole mind'). To quote C.S. Lewis once more: 'Paradoxical as it may seem, Donne's poetry is too simple to satisfy ... there is none of the depth and ambiguity of real experience in him.' Clearly those who believe Donne to be a major poet have to make a stand at this point; they have to demonstrate that Donne is, in fact, more truthfully alive to the complexity of 'real experience' than his detractors have supposed. This can only be done convincingly by means of analyses of individual poems, and to that end five of the *Songs and Sonnets* are examined in some detail later in this Commentary: 'The Sunne Rising', 'The Apparition', 'The Good-Morrow', 'Loves Alchymie', and 'The Anniversarie'. As a preliminary to these analyses, it is useful to look first at one feature for which most readers would allow that the *Songs and Sonnets* are remarkable: that is, the variety of feelings expressed in the collection as a whole.

The variety of feelings expressed in the *Songs and Sonnets* is easily established. The first poem in the first printed edition (1633) was 'The Good-Morrow', which develops out of a sense of discovery: the two lovers, their various false starts now behind them, have found together what real love is, and the poet suggests that here at last is a love that will survive even in a world dominated by change. Next comes the 'Song' written to fit an existing melody, 'Goe, and catche a falling starre': a cynical but cheerful claim that 'No where/Lives a woman true, and faire'. Third is 'Womans Constancy': the poet cites various false arguments his mistress might use to cast him off, and claims that the only reason he does not at once prove them false is that he might want to use them himself in order to reject her. The fourth poem, 'The Undertaking', is a poem of Platonic love in which the poet argues that he is among those few who can recognise and love the 'lovelinesse within', and therefore have no interest in the lesser joys of physical love. The next poem, 'The Sunne Rising', celebrates the pleasures of a satisfied love in extravagant terms: the woman is 'all States', and he, her lover, is accordingly 'all Princes', while the sun which wakes them is paltry in comparison with them. In 'The Indifferent' the poet condemns constancy in love as 'dangerous', and praises 'variety' as 'Loves sweetest Part'. The cynical note is sounded again in 'Loves Usury', but more sharply: the poet bargains with the God of Love, demanding that he be allowed now to 'travel' from one woman to another without any emotional involvement, and offering in exchange to endure in middle age even the boredom of loving someone who loves him. The eighth poem is 'The Canonization', arguing that the poet and his lady are ideally constant lovers who deserve to be worshipped as saints in the religion of love. In 'The Triple Foole' the poet mocks his own folly in (1) falling in love, (2) expressing his love in verse, and (3) thereby allowing others the opportunity to re-awaken his passion by setting his verse to music. And so it goes on throughout the collection, no one poem ever quite repeating the mood of the other.

The sense of this variety of feeling is somewhat reduced in Helen Gardner's major edition of the love poetry, where the *Songs and*

Sonnets are divided into two groups: roughly, a group collecting the more or less cynical and promiscuous poems, which are presumed to be earlier, and a group of more obviously thoughtful or idealistic poems, presumed to have been written after Donne's marriage in 1601. Yet even in this arrangement, which has not been accepted by all readers, the sense of variety is inescapable, if only because Donne's poetry draws on so many fields of reference: the bite of a flea and the music of the spheres, geography and astronomy, medieval theology and medicine, military manoeuvres, alchemy, taxation, the riddle of the Phoenix and the King's delight in hunting, all make their way into the *Songs and Sonnets*. Love, for Donne, does not exist isolated from other emotions and activities (as it does in the work of some poets), but alongside and mingled with them. Consequently, in Donne's poems love appears under many aspects, from the assurance of 'The Sunne Rising' to the anger of 'The Apparition' and the desolation of 'A Nocturnall upon S. Lucies Day'. To read the *Songs and Sonnets* through is to receive the irresistible impression that love is not one simple thing but a compound of many: 'mixt of all stuffes, paining soule, or sense', and not 'pure, and abstract' ('Loves Growth').

Many readers of Donne have wished to classify the love poems in some way; Theodore Redpath, for example, in the Introduction to his very helpful edition of the *Songs and Sonnets*, divides the poems into two main groups, according to whether the predominating attitude in them is 'negative' or 'positive', with various sub-classes within the two main categories. Redpath's arguments are reasonable, but there are possible dangers here for the unwary reader. The most obvious of these is to suppose that these groups of poems necessarily correspond to actual periods in Donne's life—for example, negative poems before his marriage, positive poems after it—when there is very little evidence to justify such a view. Still more dangerous is the assumption that each individual poem directly reflects some episode in the poet's life which was, in effect, the cause of the poem. We have no warrant, in other words, for interpreting Donne's life in terms of the poetry, or the poetry by means of what we believe we know of the life. Such an approach is in fact likely to be doubly misleading.

It is, firstly, misleading about the life to assume, say, that the cheerful cynicism of 'Womans Constancy' or 'The Flea' represents the settled attitude of Donne in his early twenties (to which period these poems are usually assigned), while the tenderness and dignity of 'A Valediction: forbidding mourning' fully represents Donne's mind in 1611 (the date Izaac Walton gave for the poem). The evidence suggests that in the mid-1590s Donne combined fashionable cynicism with genuine anxiety about his religious position, while in 1611 he was both a loving husband and a middle-aged man without a career, who had become almost desperate to secure a patron with political influence. Donne's was a complex character; his moods and interests were clearly as varied as the poems themselves, and we should not allow a desire to classify the poems to reduce and simplify our image of the man who wrote them.

The biographical approach is, secondly, likely to mislead us about the poems, and in very much the same way: that is, it tends to simplify, to flatten out the complexities within individual poems. A case in point here is **'The Sunne Rising'**. The reference to the King in the first stanza dates the poem after 1603, and, therefore, after Donne's imprudent marriage to Ann More in 1601; furthermore, the poem celebrates a completely satisfying union between two lovers who appear to dismiss the claims of the outside world, and this is a theme which may well have attracted Donne at a time when he had forfeited his post as secretary to the Lord Keeper, and was virtually an exile from the world of affairs. For many readers, unduly influenced by the romantic story of a secret marriage, the poem is simply this: a glorious surrender to the joys of sexual love as the only true reality, and a splendid denial of the significance of the outside world. But to read 'The Sunne Rising' in this way is to miss much of its richness and subtlety.

The point is most readily made by a comparison of Donne's poem with a short lyric by D.H. Lawrence (1885–1930), 'New Year's Eve':

There are only two things now,
The great black night scooped out
And this fireglow.

This fireglow, the core,
And we the two ripe pips
That are held in store.

Listen, the darkness rings
As it circulates round our fire.
Take off your things.

Your shoulders, your bruised throat!
Your breasts, your nakedness!
This fiery coat!

As the darkness flickers and dips,
As the firelight falls and leaps
From your feet to your lips!

The world here is divided starkly into two elements, each of which excludes the other; at the warm living core is the love-making of the man and the woman, and around them is an outer darkness apparently devoid of human life or value. The choice implied by the poem is correspondingly stark: love in the firelight, or extinction in the 'great black night' of the outside world. Life and growth belong only to the two lovers in the firelight; they are 'the two ripe pips/That are held in store'. The time of the poem is 'now' ('There are only two things now'), and 'now' is that moment at which the world outside the lovers can be denied as unreal, merely a 'darkness' on which they turn their backs in order to face each other. For Lawrence, at least in 'New Year's Eve', this denial of the outside world is a necessary and even integral part of the affirmation of love.

In 'The Sunne Rising' there is a similar concentration on the lovers at the warm centre, but Donne's lovers are at the centre of a living and attractive world, and the final effect of his poem is consequently very different from that of 'New Year's Eve'. Donne gives full weight to the lovers' sense that they are, uniquely, immune from time:

> Love, all alike, no season knowes, now clyme,
> Nor houres, dayes, months, which are the rags of time

and to their sense that they can afford to ignore the various claims of the world outside their bedroom:

> She'is all States, and all Princes, I,
> Nothing else is.

But Donne also admits into the poem the commonsense recognition that we all live, and love, in a world governed by time. The question in the fourth line, 'Must to thy motions lovers seasons run?', is phrased as if to invite the answer 'No', and the confidence with which the poem begins almost persuades us to give that answer. But the real answer is, of course, 'Yes', and the very presence of such a question reminds us that even the happiest lovers cannot escape being vulnerable to time and change, however arrogant or splendid their assertions to the contrary. Paradoxically, the recklessness with which Donne celebrates the idea that love is the only reality is made to carry with it an implicit confession of the absurdity of such a claim.

To describe 'The Sunne Rising' as a paradoxical poem is not to deny that its immediate appeal is extraordinary. It opens with an irresistible energy, in which we recognise not only the determination to win an argument (ostensibly with the sun, but in reality of course with the reader), but also the triumphant mood of a successful lover:

> Busie old foole, unruly Sunne,
> Why dost thou thus,
> Through windowes, and through curtaines, call on us?
> Must to thy motions lovers seasons run?
> Sawcy pedantique wretch, goe chide
> Late schoole boys, and sowre prentices,

Goe tell Court-huntsmen, that the King will ride,
Call countrey ants to harvest offices;
Love, all alike, no season knowes, nor clyme,
Nor houres, dayes, months, which are the rags of time.

This is a remarkable stanza, and we are bound to be impressed by the worldly assurance of this lover who professes to care nothing for the world. Despite his complaint that the sun has disturbed them, there is nothing sleepy about his opening outburst; he is in fact already a great deal more alert and wide-awake, indeed more 'busie', than any of those who are reluctantly setting about their day's work. And, unlike the lovers of Lawrence's 'New Year's Eve', he is evidently not tempted to retreat from the world; he is, for example, far too sure of himself to regard the sun as a possible threat to his happiness, treating it instead as an incompetent but harmless servant to be sent about his business ('goe chide', 'goe tell'). In the same brisk manner the poet scoffs at 'the rags of time' as hardly meriting the lovers' attention, since love is of its very nature 'all alike' and, therefore, exempt from the pressures of time and change. But, we notice, the poet knows precisely what time it is out there in the world he contemplates with such lordly satisfaction: it's time for schoolboys and apprentices to hurry, for courtiers to escort the King out hunting, and for farmers to begin gathering the day's harvest. In short, although the first stanza of 'The Sunne Rising' overtly denies the significance of anything outside the lovers' bedroom, it is hard to imagine ten lines which could set the lovers down more firmly in the midst of the day-to-day realities of the ordinary, familiar world.

It is, moreover, the poet's intense delight in the particular 'rag of time' the poem celebrates, a little after sunrise, that inspires the outrageous challenge to the sun's supremacy in the second stanza:

Thy beames, so reverend, and strong
Why shouldst thou thinke?
I could eclipse and cloud them with a winke

The reader may feel tempted here to intervene on behalf of the sun, by pointing out the absurd conceit of this: the poet's defiant gesture would, after all, merely leave him in the dark and the sun shining as warmly as ever. But Donne knows this perfectly well, and has his answer ready almost before we can put forward the objection:

I could eclipse and cloud them with a winke,
But that I would not lose her sight so long.

It is a marvellous moment in the poem; we can hardly continue to accuse the poet of sentimental self-deception when he has so neatly outwitted us with this unexpected reply. Donne deftly concedes that 'her sight' is revealed to him by a sun which shines with just the same brilliance for kings and schoolboys as for the lovers, and at the same time he refuses to withdraw the claim that only their love is real. The effect here is a little like that of the double-edged question in line four of the first stanza: Donne gives us the lovers' denial of the ordinary world, acknowledges the ultimate impossibility of such defiance, and continues, undisturbed, to insist on the unique reality of the lovers' experience.

Donne's manner becomes still more exuberant as he seeks to pay tribute to all that is precious about 'her sight':

> If her eyes have not blinded thine,
> Looke, and to morrow late, tell me

—a sly reminder that the sun should not repeat its mistake of intruding upon them too early—

> Whether both the'India's of spice and Myne
> Be where thou leftst them, or lie here with mee.
> Aske for those Kings whom thou sawst yesterday,
> And thou shalt heare, All here in one bed lay.

The extravagance of this is felt as a compliment to the woman. It is a way of registering the poet's sense of immeasurable contentment in her presence, a presence so richly delighting that it has converted their bedroom into a treasure-house of wealth and perfume (she is '*both* the'India's of spice *and* Myne'—not just one or the other). It would be untrue to his sense of her, we are persuaded, for Donne to speak more modestly; he needs to reach out for the most extravagant terms available to him, and the boldness with which he does so corresponds to the generosity of her gift of herself.

But there is an element of folly in all boasting, and it does not necessarily cease to appear ridiculous because it is done in verse, and by a lover. In the third stanza Donne faces this difficulty, and characteristically turns it to his advantage by carrying his extravagance to the point where it collapses:

> She'is all States, and all Princes, I,
> Nothing else is.

The two previous stanzas have been leading towards just such an effect (the question in l.4, the challenge in ll.11–14), but even so the reader is left wondering at the audacity of this; the pause which follows the short second line is filled up with our astonishment. The equivalent assertion in D.H. Lawrence's 'New Year's Eve' ('There are only two things now') leaves the reader either irritated and wanting to protest that the world we inhabit is not to be dismissed as an empty darkness, or else embarrassed at being invited to overhear the intimate talk of a lover who pretends to be unaware of our presence. 'The Sunne Rising' does not leave us feeling ill at ease in this way, essentially because Donne's boastful, loving claim is made with a recklessness that draws attention to itself, and in doing so effectively concedes the absurdity of the boast; there is, after all, a world outside the bedroom window, and its existence has been acknowledged from the first stanza onwards. Donne does indeed hint briefly that he has arguments in readiness which would prove that this world is merely an illusion:

Princes doe but *play* us; compar'd to this,
All honor's *mimique*; All wealth *alchimie*

but the whole poem has shown Donne to be so entirely at home in the world that such arguments would clearly be out of place here, and they are taken no further. Instead, Donne relaxes into a mood of humorous condescension, as the sun which had been driven from the room in the first stanza is re-admitted with a forgiving reference to its great age:

Thou sunne art half as happy'as wee,
In that the world's contracted thus;
Thine age asks ease, and since thy duties bee
To warme the world, that's done in warming us.

In the closing lines, Donne re-affirms the impossible claim of the poem, not now in the manner of one consciously defending a paradox —he has already gone as far as it is possible to go in that direction—but with a rhythm suggesting complete assurance:

Shine here to us, and thou art every where;
This bed thy center is, these walls, thy spheare.

The argumentative bustle with which the poem began, as Donne turned away from the woman to quarrel with the sun, finds its perfect answer in the poised quietness of this conclusion, as he returns to her and to the warmth of their love-making.

'The Sunne Rising', then, is more than the simple poem it is often taken to be by those who would see it as Donne's ecstatic response to his life with Ann More. That kind of simplicity is indeed to be found in Lawrence's 'New Year's Eve'. Lawrence sets up two mutually exclusive terms: the darkness of the world, and the warmth of love. Donne outdoes Lawrence in his celebration of the supreme reality of love, but he refuses to dismiss the world as merely darkness; the paradox of the poem lies in Donne's insistence that the two conflicting claims, of love and of the world, must both be met in full. It does not necessarily follow from this that one poem is more 'true' than the other —Lawrence's, we may say, leads towards an impossible denial,

Donne's towards a no less impossible affirmation—but 'The Sunne Rising', more varied in tone, more resourceful in argument, offers, perhaps, a more rewarding experience to the reader.

'The Sunne Rising', highly individual as it is, belongs to a recognised poetic tradition, that of the *aubade* or 'dawn-song'. In **'The Apparition'**, a quite different but equally characteristic poem, Donne demonstrates his individuality by interweaving two themes familiar to any reader of sixteenth-century poetry: the rejected lover's complaint that his lady's chastity is killing him, and the warning that the lady will one day long in vain for the pleasures she now refuses to grant her lover. The effect of combining the two themes is to transform them both:

> When by thy scorne, O murdresse, I am dead,
> 	And that thou thinkst thee free
> From all solicitation from mee,
> Then shall my ghost come to thy bed,
> And thee, fain'd vestall, in worse armes shall see;
> Then thy sicke taper will begin to winke . . .

The first line here apparently acknowledges the conventions of Petrarchan poetry in supposing that the rejected lover will die of unrequited love, but in every other respect this is an anti-Petrarchan poem. The lover's bitterness towards his lady is seemingly at least a match for her scorn towards him, and rather than passively lament the cruelty which is supposedly killing him, he takes a malicious pleasure in contemplating the suffering he, in his turn, will cause her. The routine poetic idea of dying for love is being used to set in motion a far from routine poem.

If the speaker is unwilling to play the part assigned by convention to the Petrarchan lover, no more is the lady quite what the Petrarchan conventions required her to be, and it soon appears that there are more straightforward charges to be brought against her than the merely customary one that she has been unkind:

> And he, whose thou art then, being tyr'd before,
> Will, if thou stirre, or pinch to wake him, thinke
> 	Thou call'st for more,
> And in false sleepe will from thee shrinke.

The 'fain'd vestall' has claimed to prize her virginity above all else in order to justify refusing herself to the would-be lover, but at her bedside his ghost will see the humiliating truth: that her sexual appetite is in fact far keener than that of the lover she has that night exhausted, and who 'shrinks' away from her in fear of further demands on his tired manhood. The lines are brutal, both in the matter-of-fact treatment of her sexual desires ('pinch', 'thinke/Thou call'st for more'), and in the suggestion that she has been casual and indiscriminate in acquiring her lovers ('in worse armes', 'he, whose thou art then'). The lines which follow allow her no respite:

And then poore Aspen wretch, neglected thou
Bath'd in a cold quicksilver sweat wilt lye
A veryer ghost than I.

This is to portray human sexuality at its most mundane, least glamorous level. It would be hard to imagine anything more remote from the elevated tone of the Petrarchan poets than this contemptuous picture of the lady sweating and trembling beside her unresponsive lover.

The poem appears to have reached its climax with these lines: the speaker has his revenge upon the lady—ignored by the lover she has accepted, and tormented by the lover she had spurned, she is still more dead-alive than he is ('A veryer ghost than I')—and at the same time he has managed to startle and amuse his readers by so thoroughly subverting the conventions of Petrarchism. But it is a part of Donne's genius that he seems always to have more to offer than the reader has anticipated. Here the unlooked-for twist comes in the last four lines:

What I will say, I will not tell thee now,
Lest that preserve thee;'and since my love is spent,
I'had rather thou shouldst painfully repent,
Than by my threatenings rest still innocent.

He declares that his love is finished ('spent'), but of course the whole basis of the poem is his continuing but hopeless desire for her. If we have been tempted to approach the poem biographically, reading it (as some have done) as if it were Donne's heartfelt outcry against a woman who had in real life refused his advances, we shall have to consider these closing lines as a blemish, a passage of futile bravado. But Donne deliberately leaves us with a mocking picture of the lover as a man who has failed during his lifetime to find words with which to woo the lady, and who is therefore reduced to threatening her with the terrible things he is sure he will be able to think of once he has died for love. These last four lines should be seen not as a slip, but as the final witty stroke in a carefully controlled poem which, without them, might appear too one-sidedly savage to be entertaining. 'The Apparition' serves as a further reminder that we should not uncritically identify the historical John Donne with the person who is made to speak in the poems.

The central image in **'The Good-Morrow'**, and the one that gives the poem its title, is that of the two lovers waking up into a new world of love. It is a brave image, and there is much that is brave and exciting about the poem: notably, the courage with which Donne seeks to acknowledge the past and the future as well as the present reality of their love, and the ambition which leads him to include so wide a range of feeling and mood in the short space of twenty-one lines. How far the courage and the ambition are eventually justified by the success of the poem *as a poem*, that is, as something which is a shaped work of art as well as a moving document of human experience, is, however, an open question.

The first few lines of 'The Good-Morrow' are often cited, quite justly, to illustrate the remarkable directness of Donne's poetic voice, so closely related to the realistic expressiveness being developed by the dramatists throughout the 1590s:

I wonder by my troth, what thou, and I
Did, till we lov'd? were we not wean'd till then?
But suck'd on countrey pleasures, childishly?
Or snorted we i'the seaven sleepers den?
'Twas so; . . .

Donne has two related tasks here: firstly, to recognise the fact that both he and she have loved before ('what *thou*, *and I*/Did'), and secondly, to insist that what they are now discovering together is at last the real world of love, and not merely another realm of 'fancies'. It would be dishonest to ignore the past; indecent to dwell on it unduly. Donne accepts it, as he must, but without alarm, and deprives it of any power to harm them by converting it into a series of comic affairs marked by hopeful enthusiasm and graceless incompetence in about equal measure. The vocabulary is at once affectionate and dismissive: 'not wean'd', 'suck'd', 'childishly', 'snorted'. The bungled 'countrey pleasures' of the past, which might have become a barrier between them, provide instead an opportunity for them to express their love in shared laughter.

But it is not easy to make the transition from laughter to affirmation. Donne is attempting, after all, to say what not only every lover but also every libertine would say: that his other women meant nothing to him in comparison with his love for her. The problem is to make the claim carry conviction:

'Twas so; But this, all pleasures fancies bee.
If ever any beauty I did see,
Which I desir'd, and got, 'twas but a dreame of thee.

We can probably pass over the rather disparaging 'any beauty', but it is more difficult to know how to respond to 'and got', an unnecessary and almost brutal aside, which seems rather to flaunt his past loves than simply to acknowledge them. What purports to be sexual honesty looks disagreeably like sexual showing-off: 'Whenever I wanted a beautiful woman, I always had her.' Such showing-off is not readily compatible with honesty, and coming where it does the smoothly reassuring "'twas but a dreame of thee' is perhaps *too* smooth to be very convincing. There is, in short, a hint of aggression here, which clashes uncomfortably with the shared amusement of the opening lines.

In the second stanza Donne turns from the past to the present. It was 'feare', we now understand, which marred the earlier effort at candour, and gave rise to the harshness of tone at the close of the first stanza. In this poem, as in a number of others ('The Anniversarie', 'A Valediction: forbidding mourning', 'A Lecture upon the Shadow'), Donne shows himself acutely aware of the possibility that love will be invaded by fear. At the same time, he seems instinctively to recognise that while we cannot banish fear, we can nonetheless rise free of it. The effect of this recognition, wherever it comes, is profoundly moving. Here, the lovely movement of the verse signals the lovers' sudden emergence from a state of suspicious watchfulness into a world of mutual contemplation, both delighted and delighting:

> And now good morrow to our waking soules,
> Which watch not one another out of feare;
> For love, all love of other sights controules,
> And makes one little roome, an every where.

By the most natural and unobtrusive of images, their literal awakening after (we assume) a night of love-making is made to suggest the awakening of their souls into a new clarity of feeling, a new certainty. It comes to them almost as a gift, to which they can respond only with wonderment, expressed in the simplest of greetings: 'And now good morrow to our waking soules'. The 'love of other sights', which might have been so damaging, has been brought calmly under control by the power of 'love' itself; so that what the lovers experience is not self-denial, or a willed limitation of self, but release, and the liberating discovery of the other:

> Let sea-discoverers to new worlds have gone,
> Let Maps to others, worlds on worlds have showne,
> Let us possesse our world, each hath one, and is one.

There is a wealth of meaning here in the word 'possesse'. It carries the suggestion both of 'self-possession', the state of mind most *un*like 'feare', and of 'sexual possession', which is so much more than the mere squandering of sexual energies the lovers had known previously ('I wonder . . . what thou, and I/*Did*'). There is, too, the further suggestion that the lovers have progressed from a lower to a higher level of existence. They 'possesse' their world, an 'every where' found without struggle in 'one little roome', and in doing so they have reached a goal denied to the explorers and astronomers who voyage across the seas or scan the heavens in search of remote 'new worlds' they can conquer or study, but never in any full sense 'possesse'. The explorers and astronomers, we may say, remain trapped in the realm of Action, while the lovers have, as if by a miracle, moved beyond them into the realm of Being.

Such terms seem especially appropriate at the beginning of the third stanza, where the mood of the lovers is one of trance-like stillness:

My face in thine eye, thine in mine appeares,
And true plaine hearts doe in the faces rest

—the deep mutual gaze, in which they each find themselves in the eyes of the other, and then the growing certainty that here at last is the complete candour which could not quite be achieved earlier in the poem. The lovers, their fears and their false starts now behind them, appear to have arrived at a point of 'rest' where all further struggle is unnecessary. But, movingly, the poem is not allowed to 'rest' here. The promise of an ideal stability leads Donne to think about the future, and immediately the note of doubt and uncertainty begins to re-appear:

Where can we finde two better hemispheares
Without sharpe North, without declining West?

The argument that their world of love will be exempt from any coldness of feeling ('sharpe North') or any falling-off of attachment ('declining West') is made to depend upon the obvious logical absurdity of a sphere consisting solely of the South and the East; the effect of the image is to suggest that permanency in love is not a real possibility, as if the world they have discovered together ('our world') were, after all, only an illusion. Donne tries an alternative argument, borrowing this time from medieval doctrines, both scientific and religious, as to the causes of disease and decay:

What ever dyes, was not mixt equally;
If our two loves be one, or, thou and I
Love so alike, that none doe slacken, none can die.

The theory behind these lines is that whatever dies or decays does so because of a lack of unity or balance in the elements of which it was composed. If, therefore, the lovers really do make up one world, or if at least their two loves are so exactly matched that there can be no decay, then there can be no death of love for them. The logic of this is, however, decidedly strained, and the possibility of a punning reference to the male orgasm ('slacken', 'die') only complicates the lines still further. It is a strange way to conclude a poem with so optimistic a title.

Two lines from another of Donne's poems, 'A Lecture upon the Shadow', help to explain what is happening in this final stanza:

Love is a growing, or full constant light;
And his first minute, after noone, is night.

The power of love to irradiate the whole experience of the lovers provides the occasion for some of the most memorable of the *Songs and Sonnets*. But if it is true that few English poets have so movingly celebrated the joys of a fulfilled love, it is also true that few others—perhaps only Shakespeare and Thomas Hardy (1840–1928)—have been so conscious of how easily a single 'minute' of doubt can darken all the mid-day brightness of love, transforming joy into despair, and mutual confidence into suspicion. The vulnerability of human love in a world dominated by time and change is a recurrent theme in the *Songs and Sonnets*, and the essential subject of 'The Good-Morrow'. None of the moods expressed in this poem is entirely stable, not even the quiet serenity of the central section. There is a brave attempt in the first stanza to dispel the fears arising from the recognition that the lovers have not always possessed their world of love, but it is only partly successful, and the poem concludes with their newly discovered clarity of feeling under threat from the fear that this world may one day be lost to them. They have not always loved each other; there may come a time when they no longer do so: this is the thought that hovers behind the last five lines of the poem. The whole conclusion is shot through with uncertainty. This is most obvious in the last two lines, where Donne is apparently unable to decide whether their 'two loves' are 'one', or merely 'alike', but there is uncertainty too in the melancholy echoing of 'none . . . none', and in the rhythm of the final line, which carries the poem haltingly to a stop on the word 'die'. Donne puts forward arguments to prove that their world of love is secure, but his arguments serve only to reveal that there can be no such proofs of security, and the poem closes on a note far removed from the vigourous confidence of the opening lines.

Not all readers of Donne will accept this account of the poem, and even among those who do accept it, there may be disagreement as to how far the poem is successful. It may be objected that Donne attempts too much in a poem of only three stanzas, and that too much is made to depend on the reader's ability to recognise and interpret the constant shifts of mood and tone. These two charges may be resolved into the larger and more general one, that the poem is just too complicated to be read with pleasure.

There is no simple answer to these objections, which were already to be heard during Donne's lifetime; a whole history of taste could be written around the question of what degree of difficulty is allowable in poetry. It is, however, broadly true that most readers of poetry in the sixteenth century expected the kinds of pleasure to be found, albeit in rather a limited way, in such a poem as 'Smooth are thy looks' (quoted in full in the Introduction, p.16): the kinds of pleasure afforded, for example, by clarity of tone and by obvious symmetries of form. Then, at the end of the century, Donne and some of his contemporaries, including Shakespeare, began to offer satisfactions of a new and different kind, by writing verse whose most notable characteristic is its imaginative truthfulness to the nature of human experience. Where that is complex, as it is in 'The Good-Morrow', the verse is correspondingly tortuous and difficult. The human experience of love is that the line which separates security from fear is extremely fragile; Donne sacrifices the formal pleasures of clarity and symmetry and the like, in order to write of the crossing and re-crossing of that line. The result is a poem of continually shifting moods, which even an experienced reader may find difficult to interpret with confidence.

In the last analysis, the question is one of different kinds of poetic pleasure. Fortunately we are not obliged to grade them, or to choose between them. Twentieth-century readers have, by and large, grown accustomed to wrestling with poetry of considerable difficulty, and this has certainly done much to ease the advance of Donne's reputation. This is all to the good, but the tendency to undervalue other and simpler forms of poetry should be resisted. The poet and critic T.S. Eliot (1888–1965), discussing the difficulty of modern poetry, suggested that 'for some periods of society a more relaxed form of writing is right, and for others a more concentrated'*. We can sensibly reapply Eliot's words, and say that what is true for some periods will equally be true for some readers. There is room in poetry for 'Smooth are thy looks' as well as for 'The Good-Morrow'.

It is a startling but instructive experience to turn from 'The Good-Morrow' to **'Loves Alchymie'**. 'The Good-Morrow' is a poem of great complexity, marked by uncertainty and by abrupt and puzzling shifts of tone, whose most moving effect is, even so, to evoke fulfilled love as a condition of absolute peace. 'Loves Alchymie' is, in contrast, the most direct of all the *Songs and Sonnets*, and utterly insistent on the impossibility of such a condition: 'Oh, 'tis imposture all'. Disillusion, anger and pain are all present in the poem, but fused together rather than treated as so many separate moods, so that the tone of the poem is one of unbroken harshness. The result is a poem of undeniable power; the critical question is to know how to respond to such a display of power.

* T.S. Eliot, *The Use of Poetry and the Use of Criticism*, Faber, London, 1933.

The imagery which opens the poem is both ugly and violent, as if Donne were mounting an assault upon the reader:

Some that have deeper digg'd loves Myne than I
Say, where his centrique happiness doth lie:
    I have lov'd, and got, and told,
But should I love, get, tell, till I were old,
I should not finde that hidden mysterie;
    Oh, 'tis imposture all.

To write of sexual love in this way is to eliminate any sense of tenderness, or indeed of any human feeling other than brutal rapacity. The woman is simply a mine to be ransacked, and the rhythm and alliteration suggest a kind of sexual stabbing ('Some that have *deeper digg'd* loves Myne than I'). The poet has 'lov'd, and got, and told', but the word 'lov'd', as it is used here, has become as empty of meaning for him as were the various women whose bodies have been plundered in the pursuit of love's 'centrique happinesse'. Successive disappointments in the search have led him only to the conviction that those who told him of the mysteries, or sacred truths of love, were liars and impostors; there is no 'hidden mysterie'. Or, if they were not deliberate cheats, then they were fools deceived by their own longings:

And as no chymique yet th'Elixer got,
    But glorifies his pregnant pot,
    If by the way to him befall
Some odoriferous thing, or med'cinall . . .

There is an extraordinary weight of contempt in these lines. Donne almost certainly has in mind the conventional literary portrayal of the alchemist as a man whose life was spent among foul smells in dark and dirty rooms; the suggestion is, then, that lover and alchemist resemble each other not only in being deluded, but also in needing the encouragement offered by the ocasional discovery of some sweeter smell than usual—'Some odoriferous thing'.

The last two lines of the stanza have the force of an epigram:

So, lovers dreame a rich and long delight,
But get a winter-seeming summers night.

The rhyme-words ('delight'/'night') provide a succinct summary of the main theme of the poem: the gulf between the warmth and happiness of which the lover dreams, and the harshness of the reality which eventually confronts him—as soon over as a summer's night, but as cold and bleak as a night in winter.

The second stanza is as embittered as the first, with the stress falling on a sense of personal despoilment. It opens with two questions, the first of which strikingly recalls the experience dramatised in Shakespeare's famous Sonnet 129, 'The expense of spirit in a waste of shame' (with which Donne's poem may usefully be compared; both poems are expressions of extreme sexual nausea, in language of extreme brutality):

> Our ease, our thrift, our honor, and our day,
> Shall we, for this vaine Bubles shadow pay?

The term 'thrift' denotes the careful management of resources, usually financial. Here, however, it is the resources of the inner self which have been wasted; peace of mind ('Our ease'), personal honour, even physical health ('our day'), have all been thrown away in a vain attempt to win a happiness which has, so the poet declares, no more substance than the shadow of a bubble.

The insistent theme of the poem is hammered out again in the following lines:

> Ends love in this, that my man,
> Can be as happy'as I can; If he can
> Endure the short scorne of a Bridegroomes play?
> That loving wretch that sweares,
> 'Tis not the bodies marry, but the mindes,
> Which he in her Angelique findes,
> Would sweare as justly, that he heares,
> In that dayes rude hoarse minstralsey, the spheares.

There is no mystery of love, and no music of the spheres to be heard by those alone whose souls have awakened; love exists only at a level so commonplace that even to think of it fills the poet with disgust ('the short scorne of a Bridegroomes play', 'that dayes rude hoarse minstralsey'). This disgust rises to a sickening climax in the final couplet:

> Hope not for minde in women; at their best
> Sweetnesse and wit, they'are but *Mummy*, possest.

'*Mummy*' was the term used for pieces of dead flesh which had been artificially preserved for the sake of their supposed medicinal value. To possess a woman sexually, then, is to enter a mindless lump of dead flesh: a revolting experience, but one which may offer temporary relief from the loss of 'ease'. The other relevant sense of 'possest' adds the equally brutal suggestion that the appearance of life in the woman—even her apparent 'Sweetnesse and wit'—comes only from the fact that the dead flesh has been possessed, or taken over, by an evil spirit or demon. The encounter with such a spirit is, according to the poet, the reality which awaits those who have pursued the dream of love as a marriage of true minds.

'Loves Alchymie' is obviously not a pleasant poem, but it is, once read, not soon forgotten, and it is difficult to know what to make of it. The difficulty is not, this time, caused by problems of interpretation, since the poem could hardly be more straightforward; nor is it simply a matter of our being disturbed by the attitudes expressed in it. Rather, it has to do with our sense that here all the powers of a considerable intelligence have been marshalled to the sole end of forcing the reader's assent. The poet has already confessed himself relentless in seeking love's 'centrique happinesse'—he has, to use his own brutal image, dug deep and often ('I have lov'd, and got, and told')—and he is no less relentless in pursuing his attack upon the illusion, as he now believes it to be, that there is some 'hidden mysterie' in love. He maintains one idea throughout the poem, in one tone of voice; no resistance is tolerated from the reader, just as none was tolerated from the women. Our difficulty with the poem is, in other words, that Donne is so obviously intent on bullying the reader into submission; 'Loves Alchymie' may be described as an example of the abuse of literary power.

There is another point which needs to be made about this poem. 'Loves Alchymie' is filled with disillusion; but where there is disillusion, there must formerly have been hope. The 'loving wretch' upon whom Donne pours such scorne in the second stanza is in fact none other than Donne himself, in such poems as 'The Extasie', where he speaks of 'Loves mysteries' (l.71), or 'A Valediction: forbidding mourning', where there is no doubting the conviction, mocked in 'Loves Alchymie', that ''Tis not the bodies marry, but the mindes':

But we by'a love, so much refin'd,
  That our selves know not what it is,
Inter-assured of the mind,
  Care lesse, eyes, lips, and hands to misse.

Here, surely, one finds the 'hidden mysterie' of love which is so fiercely denied in 'Loves Alchymie'. The force of the word 'mysterie' is to suggest that the sacred truths of love, like those of religion, cannot be commanded by the will, or won by 'digging' and 'getting'. They can, however, be *revealed*; it is just such a revelation, or sudden gift of truth, which is celebrated in the second stanza of 'The Good-Morrow'. But in that poem, as so often in the *Songs and Sonnets*, Donne is also concerned with the terrifying vulnerability of such moments of vision:

Love is a growing, or full constant light;
And his first minute, after noone, is night.
('A Lecture upon the Shadow')

'Loves Alchymie' is a poem written out of the darkness of that night which, in the *Songs and Sonnets*, is only one minute's journey from the fulfilled love of 'The Good-Morrow'. Violently opposed though the two poems are, the idealism of the one and the cynicism of the other are nonetheless the twin poles of the human experience of love in a world subject to all the pressures of time and change.

'The Anniversarie' is among the most eloquent of the *Songs and Sonnets*. It is a meditation on the lovers' sense of the timelessness of their world of love, and on the relationship of this to the world of time in which all human love necessarily takes place, and which is of course logically implied by the fact that this is a poem about the anniversary of the lovers' first meeting. The claim is that their love is immune from the pressure of time:

> This, no to morrow hath, nor yesterday,
> Running it never runs from us away,
> But truly keepes his first, last, everlasting day.

Theirs is an 'everlasting day' of love which takes them beyond any concern with 'yesterday' or 'to morrow'. But it soon becomes clear that this claim is at odds with the impetus behind the poem, which is, firstly, to celebrate the fact that they have now enjoyed a whole year of yesterdays together, and secondly, to anticipate a series of equally happy tomorrows—a series which, Donne is later to admit, no amount of good faith or good fortune can possibly make '*ever*lasting' (albeit the lovers can hope that nothing less than the limits of life itself will bring their days together to an end). In short, to celebrate an 'Anniversarie' (literally a 'returning yearly') is also to concede that even lovers have to submit to the world of time.

There is, clearly, a strong thematic resemblance between 'The Anniversarie' and 'The Sunne Rising':

> Love, all like, no season knowes, nor clyme,
> Nor houres, dayes, months, which are the rags of time.

But 'The Anniversarie' is an altogether quieter poem, the tone sober rather than delightedly paradoxical. The opening lines request our attention instead of demanding it:

> All Kings, and all their favorites,
> All glory'of honors, beauties, wits,
> The Sun it selfe, which makes times, as they passe,
> Is elder by a yeare, now, than it was
> When thou and I first one another saw.

The poem begins as if Donne is preparing to acclaim the mighty ones of the earth—the kings and their favourites, the honoured, the beautiful, the clever—but the verse sweeps on, and it becomes clear that they are mentioned in order that he may record that they, too, are moving on towards their graves. Even the sun, customarily the symbol of all that is glorious and powerful, is presented not as the monarch of the temporal world but as its chief victim, making times only to be itself made older by them, 'as they passe'. There is no place here for the mocking laughter directed against 'the rags of time' in 'The Sunne Rising'. Instead, the transience of all things is acknowledged, with measured calmness, as one of the central facts of human existence.

But here, as always in the *Songs and Sonnets*, the lovers must make a stand against the power of time:

All other things, to their destruction draw,
  Only our love hath no decay;
This, no to morrow hath, nor yesterday,
Running it never runs from us away,
But truly keepes his first, last, everlasting day.

The steady movement of the verse invites us to consider where the stresses should fall, and, no matter how we may eventually decide to hear the lines, to allow at least some weight to the alternatives. We need to be aware, in other words, both of the emphatic '*All* other things . . . ' followed by the timid daring of '*Only* our love . . . ', and of the more dismissive 'All *other things* . . . ' followed by the bold pride of 'Only *our love* hath *no* decay'. The one reading seems to concede too much, and the other too little, to the universal drawing-on towards destruction; our sense that both readings are required is an indication of the difficulties Donne faces in dealing with the theme of an anniversary.

There is is another way to describe these difficulties. The essential impulse behind the poem is one which is entirely familiar in life as in literature: the lover's wish to say 'I will love you for ever.' But it is obvious that an element of falseness generally attaches to such declarations; to the extent that we are all not only mortal but changeable—liable, in fact, to 'decay' as well as to 'destruction'—we need to be extremely wary about how we lay claim to 'for ever'. Once we have recognised this, we may feel obliged to judge all such avowals severely, as a species of dishonesty, or at the least to agree with Samuel Johnson in seeing them as evidence of human folly; vows, he wrote (in a note on Shakespeare's play, *Love's Labour's Lost*), 'proceed commonly from a presumptuous confidence, and a false estimate of human powers'. But there is surely something else that also needs to be recognised: that an increased confidence, and an enlarged estimate of human powers, are among the necessary conditions for love to exist at all; for without these, love would be cancelled almost before it began by the fear and watchfulness of which Donne writes, for example, in 'The Good-Morrow'. The avowal Donne makes in this poem, 'Only our love hath no decay', is both impossible (all things draw on towards destruction), and inevitable (without such a conviction love cannot exist); the great achievement of 'The Anniversarie' is that in it Donne is able to find a point of balance between the presumptuous (but wonderfully exhilarating) confidence of 'The Sunne Rising', and the almost paralysing loss of confidence felt in the concluding lines of 'The Good-Morrow'.

In the opening stanza of 'The Anniversarie' Donne affirms the 'first, last, everlasting day' of their love—'first' and 'last' as it were denied and overthrown by 'everlasting'. But 'first' and 'last' are not to be dismissed so easily: there was a time when they 'first one another saw', and there will come a time when they have to leave each other 'at last in death'. The thought of death thrusts itself forward in the second stanza:

> Two graves must hide thine and my corse,
> If one might, death were no divorce.

The fact is stated with the utmost simplicity; they will both die, and be buried (in separate graves, so presumably they are not husband and wife). This simplicity looks for a moment like calm acceptance of what is, after all, the common lot of mankind:

> Alas, as well as other Princes, wee
> (Who Prince enough in one another bee,)
> Must leave at last in death, these eyes, and eares,
> Oft fed with true oathes, and with sweet salt teares

In his sonnet on the death of his wife ('Since she whome I lovd, hath payd her last debt'), Donne maintains a calm so fixed and severe that the reader can only wonder at the strength of the feeling which is being suppressed, and at the still stronger will which suppresses it; Donne's editor, Helen Gardner, finds the poem at one point 'almost intolerably harsh'. The calm of 'The Anniversarie' is, however, less rigid, and it seems to falter a little as Donne lingers on the felt physical presence of the woman before him, whose sight, taste, touch, will all be lost to him with her death ('these eyes, and eares,/Oft fed with true oathes, and with sweet salt teares'). The last four lines of the stanza are a search for consolation:

> But soules where nothing dwells but love
> (All other thoughts being inmates) then shall prove
> This, or a love increased there above,
> When bodies to their graves, soules from their graves remove.

These lines, like those which conclude 'The Good-Morrow', are not entirely clear, and in both cases the confusion arises for much the same reasons. Donne's argument seems to be that love alone 'dwells' in their souls, while their 'other thoughts' are merely 'inmates': that is, passing thoughts, or thoughts which are present in their souls without properly belonging to them. Death will dislodge these 'inmates' from their souls, and this will leave the lovers free to enjoy 'a love increased there above'. Accordingly, death can be seen as providing a means of release from the limitations of life. No doubt this is one way of coming to terms with the fact of death, but it does not carry much conviction in the poem, partly because the distinction between *dwelling* and *being an inmate* seems somewhat flimsy and uncertain, and partly because Donne is so obviously *not* content to regard the woman's body as no more than the grave of her soul—'these eyes, and eares' are too intimately known, too precious to him, for such a piece of piety to afford any genuine consolation. The religious argument is brought in to buttress the lovers' claims to an 'everlasting day' of shared love, but the effect of the stanza as a whole is to suggest once again the intensity with which Donne fears the everlasting night of utter separateness.

The third stanza begins as if Donne is planning to build upon the unstable foundations of the second, but just as it seems Donne has gained his point, the argument is unexpectedly dropped, as though the support it offered were no longer what was needed:

> And then wee shall be throughly blest,
> But wee no more, than all the rest.

They will be completely happy ('throughly blest') in the next world, but that will be 'then' and 'there above', and all the evidence of the second stanza is that the lovers are unwilling to set aside the happiness available to them here and now, in this world. Moreover, 'there above' the lovers will be 'no more, than all the rest'; they will have lost their sense of being peculiarly and supremely blessed in their love. It is not so in this world:

> Here upon earth, we'are Kings, and none but wee
> Can be such Kings, nor of such subjects bee.

—they alone can be Kings over such subjects as themselves, and they alone can be subjects under such Kings as each other. There is more assurance here than in the second stanza—they are 'Kings' now, not merely 'Prince enough in one another' ('Prince *enough*': that is, not really Princes at all)—but this is still far removed from the exuberance and recklessness of 'The Sunne Rising'. The assertion of the lovers' supremacy is made to include the admission that theirs is, after all, a kingdom of only two—which is modest indeed, beside 'She'is all States, and all Princes, I,/Nothing else is'—and Donne pauses to consider the grimmer implications of a royalty to be enjoyed 'Here upon earth':

> Who is so safe as wee? where none can doe
> Treason to us, except one of us two.

'*Except one of us two*': 'treason' may cut short the royal life extended to each of them by their mutual love. He may betray her; or she may betray him. This chilling thought, like the fear of their eventual divorce in death, has also to be acknowledged between them.

This is the critical moment in the poem. They could face 'destruction' together, but the prospect of love's 'decay' can only come between them, compelling them against their wills to 'watch . . . one another out of feare' ('The Good-Morrow'). The thought cannot be simply denied, because there are true as well as false fears in love, and to insist otherwise would itself be false; but, whether true *or* false, such fears are demeaning, and to give way to them, to allow them to take hold over their imaginations, would be to dishonour their status as lovers. Donne meets the crisis with memorable dignity:

> True and false feares let us refraine,
> Let us love nobly,'and live, and adde againe
> Yeares and yeares unto yeares, till we attaine
> To write threescore: this is the second of our raigne,

With these lines the inevitable limitations of human life are finally accepted, but accepted bravely. They cannot banish their fears of death or betrayal, because such fears are among the ordinary conditions of our existence, but they can 'refraine' them, keep them under control. To do so will be to 'love nobly': for what could be more *ig*noble for them than to live in continual fear of some future act of infidelity? Only by refusing to be deterred by fear can they make good their pretensions to royalty in love, and therefore 'live': that is, embrace their happiness here upon earth, rather than wait in timorous expectation of happiness in heaven. If their love cannot in truth be endless, they can still 'attaine/To write threescore', and thereby achieve a triumph not *over* time but *in* time. Instead of being daunted by the passing of the years, they will use them as the measure of their fulfilment: 'this is the second of our *raigne*'.

All this is markedly different from the claims advanced in the first stanza. Their initial aspiration was towards an 'everlasting day' of love, floating free of yesterdays and tomorrows, but this has been gradually let go during the course of the poem: the lovers who began by denying time end by resolving to immerse themselves in it to the full, adding 'Yeares and yeares unto yeares'. But while the original claim has been surrendered, the poem has brought them to a fuller realisation of what can justly be celebrated in a poem about an anniversary: the nobility of a love enjoyed here in the world where they 'first one another saw'.

Part 4

Hints for study

THERE IS NO SHORT AND EASY WAY to become master of Donne's poetry; but, on the other hand, the poems are not necessarily so difficult to understand and enjoy as is sometimes supposed. There are only two pieces of essential advice: first, always to consider each poem separately; and second, always to begin by reading the poem in question aloud.

To take the first point, first: always consider each poem separately. Do not be too eager to establish generalisations about Donne's work as a whole, or to divide the poems into groups according to mood or theme, or to seize on one poem as so central or so characteristic that it can be made to provide a 'key' to all the others. While such approaches may seem to promise clarity, they lead almost inevitably to distortions —for example, to think of the poems as falling into groups is often to overlook the fact that Donne tackles the same theme with different degrees of success in different poems.

In learning how to confront each of Donne's poems individually and, as it were, in its own right, the inexperienced reader can hardly do better than hold in mind a phrase used by F.R. Leavis (in *Revaluation*, Chatto and Windus, London, 1936), celebrating Donne's 'irresistible rightness of tone', and then go on to ask a series of related questions about each poem. Firstly, about its 'rightness': what is it that Donne is trying to be right *about*, and how successful is he? Secondly, about the 'tone': what lies behind, and what is the effect of, the tone—more often, the changes of tone—in a given poem? In one way or another, these are the questions that were discussed in the accounts of individual poems in Part 3 of these Notes, and there is no more valuable exercise the student can undertake at this point than to make use of the same questions in order to give a similar account of (say) 'Loves Growth' or 'A Valediction: forbidding mourning'.

The second piece of advice is no less essential than the first: always begin by reading the poems aloud. The seeming irregularity of Donne's rhythmic effects has been a source of difficulty to many readers; Samuel Johnson thought it was possible to recognise metaphysical verse as verse 'only . . . by counting the syllables'. In fact, Donne is reasonably regular in terms of syllable count, and the basic pulse of his verse is clearly iambic (for example, in 'The Will': 'To hím for whóm the pássing béll next tólls,/I leáve my phýsick bóokes . . . '), but it would in truth be a task of all but endless complexity to devise a system of formal rules which would explain how we should read each and every line of Donne's verse. At the cost of some simplification, the problem may be presented thus: the iambic line is felt to be regular when the difference in weight betweeen the alternate unstressed and stressed syllables is strongly marked, as it was in most Elizabeth verse, and as it was to be again from (roughly) the later seventeenth century until the close of the nineteenth. But while Donne is occasionally regular in this way, as in the lines just quoted, he often gives more weight to the notionally unstressed syllables than most of his contemporaries would have expected, or, in some cases, tolerated. The reader of most Elizabethan verse grows accustomed to moving in a series of gentle steps, as if across a level lawn:

One day I wrote her name upon the strand,
  but came the waves and washèd it away:
  agayne I wrote it with a second hand,
  but came the tyde, and made my paynes his pray . . .
(Edmund Spenser, *Amoretti*, Sonnet LXXV, 1595)

But in many of Donne's poems the words are packed together like boulders along a rocky coast-line, and the reader has to learn how to clamber from one to another, as in 'A Nocturnall upon S. Lucies Day':

All others, from all things, draw all that's good.
Life, soule, forme, spirit, whence they beeing have;
  I, by loves limbecke, am the grave
  Of all, that's nothing. Oft a flood
    Have wee two wept, and so
Drownd the whole world, us two; oft did we grow
To be two Chaosses, when we did show
Care to ought else; and often absences
Withdrew our soules, and made us carcasses.

Fortunately, a note made in 1811 by the poet and critic Samuel Taylor Coleridge (1772–1834) provides all the help that is necessary: full use should be made of 'pause, hurrying of voice, or apt and sometimes double emphasis', and the aim should always be to 'bring out the sense of passion more prominently'. In other words, an understanding of the *drama* of the verse will almost always guide the reader to an understanding of its rhythmic character; and, correspondingly, to discover how to read the verse aloud will almost always afford clues to an understanding of its logic and structure.

Examination topics and specimen answers

The questions examiners regularly ask about Donne's poetry may be divided for convenience into three groups, each with its associated pitfalls. Examples of each kind of question are discussed below, followed by a specimen question and answer.

1. Questions about the formal characteristics of Donne's verse

Into this category come questions about poetic techniques (for example, use of imagery, different verse forms, rhythmic effects), and questions about Donne's place in the history of literature and literary criticism. For example:

(*a*) How would you reply to Ben Jonson's charge that 'for not keeping of accent Donne deserved hanging'?
(*b*) One contemporary described Donne as 'a great writer of conceited verses'. Discuss Donne's use of the conceit.

To answer these questions it is clearly essential to understand the terms used in them: you cannot attempt (*a*), for example, if you do not recognise it as a question about the way Donne handles rhythm. (The advice given above, on pp.89–90, on reading the poems aloud, will be found useful in answering questions on this subject.)

With regard to, (*b*), there are three terms in particular with which you need to be familiar: *metaphysical*, *wit*, and *conceit*. We owe the word *metaphysical* as a critical term initially to the poet John Dryden, who complained that Donne 'affects the metaphysics, not only in his satires, but in his amorous verses, where nature only should reign': in other words, Donne employs the language of philosophical speculation ('metaphysics') in contexts where it seemed to Dryden affected and inappropriate. Samuel Johnson took up Dryden's word and extended the charge in his 'Life of Cowley' (1779), which remains to this day the only item of secondary reading which every student of Donne needs to consult. Johnson classed together a number of writers, including Donne, as 'the metaphysical poets'. Their common failing, according to Johnson, was that they had forsaken the true business of the poet, which was to represent either human nature or the natural world in such a way as to call upon the deepest feelings of the reader, and had instead written only in order to show off their unusual learning and their intellectual ingenuity—that is, their *wit*. Johnson found his evidence in the delight taken by these writers in the discovery of improbable and even fantastic points of comparison between things at first sight utterly unlike each other; such comparisons, when elaborated and made part of the argument of the poem, are known as *conceits*. Johnson provides several examples from the *Songs and*

Sonnets: the comparison of the lover's tears to the world in 'A Valediction: of Weeping' (ll.10–18), and—the most often discussed of all metaphysical conceits—Donne's comparison of the continuing relationship of two lovers, even when parted, to the interdependent movements of the legs of a pair of compasses, in the last three stanzas of 'A Valediction: forbidding mourning'. Johnson's apparent belief that such passages of wit must necessarily detract from the seriousness and emotional power of the poems in which they occur has been challenged in the present century, in particular by T.S. Eliot in essays on 'The Metaphysical Poets' and on 'Andrew Marvell' (both first published in 1921, and reprinted in *Selected Essays*, Faber, London, 1932; enlarged edition 1951). Most critics have, however, been prepared to follow Johnson in regarding the use of such conceits as the defining characteristic of metaphysical poetry.

What does it mean to describe Donne as 'a metaphysical poet'?

Donne did not call himself a 'metaphysical poet', nor did he write a 'manifesto of metaphysical verse', so there is room for argument about the meaning of the term. It is possible, however, to identify certain features of Donne's verse as characteristic of Donne in particular and of metaphysical poetry in general.

The first of these is the use of the conceit: that is, a comparison which is more obviously ingenious than either true or appropriate. The most famous example in Donne's poetry is his elaborate comparison of two lovers to the legs of a pair of compasses in 'A Valediction: forbidding mourning', but the conceit may also appear in simpler and briefer forms, as in 'The Extasie':

> Loves mysteries in soules doe grow,
> But yet the body is his booke.

Sometimes a whole poem may be seen as the working out in detail of one central conceit, as is the case with 'The Flea', where Donne argues from the fact that the flea has bitten them both to the conclusion that 'wee almost, nay more than maryed are', or with 'Loves Alchymie', where the main conceit is that the lover who seeks love's 'hidden mysterie' is as deluded as the alchemist who seeks the elixir of life.

In all of these cases, because the point of the comparison is not obvious, it has to be proved. Consequently, many metaphysical poems, and most of Donne's, have an argumentative, or at least an apparently logical structure. A good example is 'Loves Growth', where Donne's argument that love is 'elemented' rather than 'pure' is developed through a series of seemingly logical stages, the connections marked by 'But if . . . ', 'And yet . . . ', 'If . . . ', 'For . . . ', 'As . . . '.

Similarly, 'The Good-Morrow' moves logically from past to present to future, and numerous other poems have at least the appearance of a logical structure, even when Donne flouts all logical rules in order to arrive at his conclusions: 'Loves Growth', for example, begins by admitting that love is liable to change, but ends by denying this.

Two other characteristic features of metaphysical poetry, including Donne's, are closely related to this use of a quasi-logical structure. One is that the poems are often compressed and difficult. Each line is intended to help the argument of the poem, and the reader is not allowed to relax. There is very little writing which is purely ornamental or descriptive in metaphysical poetry. The other is that the diction of metaphysical poetry is usually intellectual rather than sensuous. This is especially true of Donne, who favours words that are moral or evaluative rather than descriptive or evocative (that is, 'true', 'false', 'good', 'bad', rather than 'soft' or 'sweet'). Both these points may be illustrated from 'The Good-Morrow', where we are not told what colour the lady's eyes are, or how lovely she is, but are instead asked to think about 'True plaine hearts' and about the possibility of permanency in love in a world of change.

The other leading characteristic of metaphysical verse, including Donne's, is its dramatic quality. Donne's poetry is dramatic in two senses. Firstly, most of the poems, both secular and divine, seem to arise out of particular situations—a man and a woman waking up in bed together, or celebrating an anniversary, or compelled to part, or a man confronting his God as he faces serious illness or the thought of damnation. Secondly, the language and movement of the verse are dramatic in that they are vivid, colloquial, and often suggestive of the rhythms of ordinary speech. The obvious examples are the opening lines of various poems ('For Godsake hold your tongue, and let me love', 'Busie old foole, unruly Sunne'), but the point holds good for almost all of Donne's poetry.

One last point may be made about the features noted here as characteristic of Donne in particular and of metaphysical poetry in general. To stress the dramatic element in Donne, as most modern readers do, is to emphasise the human interest of the verse. Yet this quality is exactly what Samuel Johnson felt was obscured by the use of the conceit; Johnson could not believe in the grief of a poet who compared his tears to coins, or parted lovers to a pair of compasses. Metaphysical poetry, including Donne's, constantly raises the question of the relation of the witty conceit to the emotional interest of a poem, but this is a general question to which there can be no general answer. In effect, Johnson is sometimes wrong, sometimes right. In describing Donne as a 'metaphysical poet', then, it should not be forgotten that metaphysical poetry is not all the same, and in the last analysis the differences between poems may matter far more than the features they have in common. 'Loves Growth' is not more typical of metaphysical poetry than, for example, 'The Will', but it is surely a far greater poem.

2. Questions about the themes and attitudes of Donne's poetry

For example:
(*a*) Consider how far it is useful to divide the *Songs and Sonnets* into groups according to the attitudes expressed in them.
(*b*) Discuss the question of Donne's 'sincerity' in the *Songs and Sonnets* OR in the *Divine Poems*.
(*c*) 'Donne is more interested in love itself than in any loved person.' Would you agree with this view?

Most students find questions about the themes and attitudes of Donne's poetry easier and more enjoyable than those about its formal characteristics. Unfortunately, too much enthusiasm is sometimes as damaging to an essay as too little knowledge. You may, for example, feel tempted by (*b*) to describe the central place of sincerity in your own view of personal relationships; but the examiner will already have his or her own estimate of the value of sincerity, and is concerned only with what you have to say in direct answer to a question about Donne's verse. Concentrate on the task in hand, which is to write clearly and intelligently about Donne; you will find, if you do so, that your essays carry the impress of your own individuality far more effectively than if you set out to use them as a means of personal expression.

Do the *Songs and Sonnets*, taken as a whole, constitute a 'lecture . . . in love's philosophy'?

It is impossible to determine whether Donne intended to express a philosophy of love in the *Songs and Sonnets*, but it seems unlikely. The poems were written over a long period of time, perhaps as much as twenty years, and Donne's attitudes no doubt changed a good deal during this period. However, there are a number of points which can be made about the view of love which emerges from the *Songs and Sonnets*, even if these points do not, in fact, add up to a 'philosophy'.

One point which has to be made at the outset is that there are many different kinds of relationship described or implied in these poems. The assumption in 'The Flea', for example, is that the only thing which matters is sexual satisfaction; the poem is a battle of wits, and the prize is the woman's presumed surrender to the poet's demands. In contrast to this is 'A Valediction: forbidding mourning', where the poet scorns 'Dull sublunary lovers love/(Whose soule is sense)', and celebrates a love so 'refin'd' that mere physical absence cannot diminish its perfection.

Both the scorn for 'sublunary lovers love', and the insistence that true love is attainable only by a select few, are repeated in other poems, for example in 'The Extasie' and in 'The Canonization'. In both of these poems Donne speaks of love as a 'mysterie'. This is to suggest that love is a sacred state, which so exalts the lovers that they can claim to be a 'world' to themselves, and immune to the pressures of time and change. This idea of the self-sufficiency of the lovers is part of the argument of both 'The Good-Morrow' and 'The Sunne Rising', for example, in which the lovers set out to defy time, just as in 'A Valediction: forbidding mourning' they defy distance.

In many of the *Songs and Sonnets*, however, including 'The Anniversarie' as well as the poems just cited, the claim for the lovers' supremacy over the temporal world is accompanied by an acute sense of their vulnerability in a world dominated by time. The bravado of 'The Sunne Rising' cannot blind us to the fact that the sun will rise and set regardless of the lover's boasts, and in 'The Anniversarie' the lovers' conviction that 'Here upon earth, we'are Kings' cannot obscure the fact that, at the last, 'Two graves must hide thine and my corse'. There is, too, always the fear of betrayal ('*If* our two loves be one . . . none can die'), and it is hard not to feel that the cynicism of 'Loves Alchymie' derives from the memory of some such breach of faith. In this poem at least Donne is himself part of that despised 'layetie' which fails to see the 'mysterie' of love: 'Oh, 'tis imposture all'. Love in the *Songs and Sonnets* may be 'so much refin'd,/That our selves know not what it is', but it still has to subsist in the ordinary or 'sublunary' world.

In a few poems (notably 'Loves Growth', 'Aire and Angels', and 'The Extasie') Donne does address himself directly to a philosophical question: that of the relation of body and soul in love. The argument of all three poems is that love is not 'pure' but 'elemented': that is to say, the mind and body are, if not equal, at least equally necessary to a full human love. Thus in 'The Extasie' the body is not seen as 'drosse', or waste material to be discarded, but as 'allay': an element of little account on its own, but one which increases the strength of the whole compound. Donne's conclusion is that the loving self is hindered, and 'a great Prince in prison lies', unless body and soul can work together in harmony.

'The Extasie', then, contradicts both 'The Flea' (which ignores the spiritual element in love) and 'The Undertaking' (which denies the physical element, the 'Hee and Shee'). The only way, therefore, to construct a coherent 'philosophy of love' from the *Songs and Sonnets* is to emphasise some poems at the expense of others; since this would obviously be improper, it seems better not to look for a carefully composed 'lecture . . . in love's philosophy', but to accept that Donne expressed different attitudes in different poems according to the mood of the moment. At the same time, however, it may be said that so many of the *Songs and Sonnets* assert the dignity of love, and its claim on the entire self—both body and soul—that it seems reasonable to think that it is in these poems that the reader comes closest to discovering Donne's usual feelings about love.

3. Questions about the general character of Donne's poetry

For example:
(*a*) According to C.S. Lewis, 'Donne's real limitation is not that he writes *about*, but that he writes *in*, a chaos of violent and transitory passions.' Do you accept this view?
(*b*) It has been said that the most notable feature of metaphysical poetry is its 'robust delight in dialectic'. Is this true of Donne's poetry?
(*c*) Would you agree with F.R. Leavis, that Donne is 'obviously a living poet in the most important sense'?

The typical question in this category takes the form of an invitation to discuss a general characterisation of the nature of Donne's poetry, or a general assessment of his success or failure as a poet. It is essential here to adopt a proper attitude towards the quoted comment. You need not be *too* deferential: if critics as distinguished as F.R. Leavis and C.S. Lewis can disagree, there is certainly room for disagreement, and you should feel free to present your argument even if this means challenging their authority. You must not be *at all* discourteous: professional academics do not always set a good example, but remember that there is nothing to be gained from attacking the integrity or the intelligence of critics who may, in some instances, have influenced the attitudes towards poetry of an entire generation of readers. You should, in short, treat any comment quoted in a question as firmly as you think necessary, but also with respect.

Do you think J.B. Leishman's phrase 'the dialectical* expression of personal drama' a useful characterisation of what is to be found in Donne's poetry?

The readiest way to establish the appropriateness of this phrase is to examine Leishman's three main terms one by one: 'dialectical', 'personal', and 'drama'.

* 'Dialectical', here, means 'having the character of a logical argument'.

Leishman was clearly right to point to the dialectical or argumentative character of many of Donne's poems. The nature of the argumentation varies from instance to instance. It can be outrageous, as when Donne argues for the lovers' supremacy over the sun ('The Sunne Rising'), or that the woman's loss of her virginity is of no more account than the bite of a flea ('The Flea'). In both cases, part of the pleasure of the poem derives from the reader's sense of being outwitted by a master disputant. On other occasions Donne's arguments are more demanding. In the case of 'Aire and Angels', for example, the poem as a whole is organised dialectically, in that Donne considers and rejects two contrasting accounts of love before he moves on to propose his own by means of the conceit which gives the poem its title; but to appreciate the force of this conceit, in which air is to angels what women's love is to men's love, is itself an exercise in dialectics. 'Aire and Angels' is perhaps an extreme example in this respect, but Donne almost always uses the conceit in order to win an argument or to reach a conclusion, and to the extent that his is a conceited poetry, it is also, by that very fact, dialectical in character.

In order to describe Donne's poetry as the 'expression of personal drama', it is necessary to distinguish between poetry which is *personal* and poetry which is *autobiographical*. The impress of Donne's personality is on all that he wrote, but in only a few instances is it possible to be confident that he was writing directly from his own experience. (A case in point is the sonnet 'Since she whome I lovd', which surely refers to the death in 1617 of Ann Donne.) It is possible that 'The Apparition', for example, had its origin in some event in Donne's life, but it is equally possible that it was written as an exercise in the anti-Petrarchan manner to amuse a few friends; Donne himself said that he did best when he had least truth for his subject. This being said, there is of course a sense in which the word 'personal' comes naturally to the mind of any reader of Donne. The poems are written in the first person, and the first person pronouns recur again and again in virtually every poem: 'I have done one braver thing', 'I long to talke with some old lovers ghost ', 'This is my playes last scene'. In this sense, but only in this sense, Leishman's word must be allowed to stand.

Leishman is also right to emphasise the dramatic character of Donne's poetry. The language is dramatic, in that it is vivid and colloquial, and the rhythms of normal speech are felt pressing against the basic iambic pulse, as is also the case in most Shakespearean dramatic verse. Furthermore, almost all of the poems, secular and divine, seem to arise out of particular situations—two lovers waking up in bed together, or obliged to take leave of each other—or at least it brings particular situations before the reader's imagination, as in 'The Apparition', or in the majority of the 'Divine Meditations'.

Leishman's brief characterisation of Donne's poems as 'the dialectical expression of personal drama' is, then, fair and apt. It does, however, blur the distinction between different kinds of drama in Donne's poetry. 'The Flea', for example, is dramatic in the senses outlined above, but the situation in the poem is interesting to Donne only as the means to a variety of witty effects. Poems like 'The Anniversarie' or 'The Good-Morrow', on the other hand, are dramatic in a further sense of the word. The shifts of tone and mood in these poems represent the speaker's changing understanding of the situation in which the lovers find themselves (for example, the second stanza of 'The Anniversarie', beginning 'Two graves must hide thine and my corse', reflects the speaker's recognition that even the 'everlasting day' of love may be vulnerable to time). The real drama of these poems, in other words, lies in the exploration of human feelings about love. 'The Flea' is dramatic much as any virtuoso performance before an audience is dramatic, while 'The Anniversarie' is dramatic in the manner of a play such as Shakespeare's *Anthony and Cleopatra*. To make this point is not to deny the usefulness of Leishman's phrase, but only to show that no brief characterisation of a poet as complex as Donne can possibly be entirely satisfactory.

Part 5

Suggestions for further reading

Editions of Donne's poetry

GARDNER, HELEN (ED.): *John Donne: The Divine Poems*, Clarendon Press, Oxford, 1952. The standard scholarly edition, with full textual notes.

GARDNER, HELEN (ED.): *John Donne: The Elegies and the Songs and Sonnets*, Clarendon Press, Oxford, 1965. The standard scholarly edition of the love poetry, with full texual notes.

GRIERSON, H.J.C., (ED.): *The Poems of John Donne*, 2 volumes, Clarendon Press, Oxford, 1912. For forty years the standard edition of Donne's poems, and still of great value.

REDPATH, T., (ED.): *The Songs and Sonnets of John Donne*, Methuen, London, 1956. A full and helpful annotation: now available in a paperback edition.

SMITH, A.J., (ED.): *John Donne: The Complete English Poems*, Penguin Books, Harmondsworth, 1971. The fullest and most fully annotated one-volume edition of the poems. The text is slightly modernised: useful bibliography.

Biographies of Donne

A number of the critical studies listed below include some biographical information; the standard life of Donne is R.C. Bald, *John Donne: A Life*, Clarendon Press, Oxford, 1970.

Critical studies

In an ideal world, the student coming to Donne for the first time might make his or her way through the following studies in turn, before embarking on any of the more specialised and often highly detailed scholarly discussions:

WINNY, JAMES: *A Preface to Donne*, Longman, London, 1970; revised, 1981. This contains much useful information on the life and background, and discussions of a number of poems by Donne and his contemporaries.

LEWIS, C.S.: 'Donne and Love Poetry in the Seventeenth Century', and BENNETT, JOAN, 'The Love Poetry of John Donne: A Reply to Mr. C.S. Lewis', both originally in J. DOVER WILSON (ED.), *Seventeenth-Century Studies Presented to Sir Herbert Grierson*, Clarendon Press, Oxford, 1938; also available in W.R. KEAST (ED.), *Seventeenth-Century English Poetry*, Oxford University Press, New York, 1962

JOHNSON, SAMUEL: 'The Life of Cowley', in J.P. HARDY (ED.), *Johnson's Lives of the Poets: A Selection*, Oxford University Press, Oxford, 1971. Johnson's brief discussion of 'metaphysical poetry' remains the one account of Donne and his supposed followers that every student of Donne needs to consider.

ELIOT, T.S.: 'The Metaphysical Poets' and 'Andrew Marvell', both reprinted in T.S. ELIOT, *Selected Essays*, Faber, London, 1932; revised edition, 1951. Eliot takes up Johnson's view that 'wit' is at odds with poetic seriousness in two brief essays; in espousing Donne, Eliot helped to bring about a revolution in taste which made Donne one of the most admired of English poets.

LEAVIS, F.R.: 'The Line of Wit', in *Revaluation*, Chatto and Windus, London, 1936. Leavis was one of the first academic critics to develop Eliot's arguments, and *Revaluation* one of the most influential of modern critical studies.

SANDERS, WILBUR: *John Donne's Poetry*, Cambridge University Press, Cambridge, 1971. Sanders continues the argument between Johnson and Eliot, and in doing so produces perhaps the most sympathetic and persuasive of all the studies of Donne's love poetry; the discussion of the religious poems is less satisfactory, perhaps, but still rewarding.

LEISHMAN, J.B.: *The Monarch of Wit*, Hutchinson, London, 1951. Leishman's study, though less lively than that of Sanders, covers much of the ground that any student needs to consider.

CAREY, JOHN: *John Donne: Life, Mind, and Art*, Faber, London, 1981. An ambitious and wide-ranging study, suitable only to the student who is already well informed about Donne.

CRUTTWELL, P.: *The Shakespearean Moment* Chatto and Windus, London, 1954, and 'The Love Poetry of John Donne: Pedantique Weeds or Fresh Invention', in M. BRADBURY and D. PALMER (EDS.), *Metaphysical Poetry*, Arnold, London, 1970. The discussion of Donne in *The Shakespearean Moment*, as well as the later essay, have the great merit of sending the reader back to the poems with renewed vigour.

The author of these notes

PHILLIP MALLETT read English at King's College, Cambridge, where he was sometime Charles Oldham Shakespeare Scholar of the University, and graduated with first-class honours in 1968. After a year spent teaching at Trent College in Nottinghamshire, he returned to Cambridge to do post-graduate work on the writings of John Ruskin. Since 1972 he has been a Lecturer in English at the University of St Andrews.

YORK NOTES

The first 250 titles

	Series number
CHINUA ACHEBE	
A Man of the People	(116)
Arrow of God	(92)
Things Fall Apart	(96)
ELECHI AMADI	
The Concubine	(139)
ANONYMOUS	
Beowulf	(225)
JOHN ARDEN	
Serjeant Musgrave's Dance	(159)
AYI KWEI ARMAH	
The Beautyful Ones Are Not Yet Born	(154)
JANE AUSTEN	
Emma	(142)
Mansfield Park	(216)
Northanger Abbey	(1)
Persuasion	(69)
Pride and Prejudice	(62)
Sense and Sensibility	(91)
HONORÉ DE BALZAC	
Le Père Goriot	(218)
SAMUEL BECKETT	
Waiting for Godot	(115)
SAUL BELLOW	
Henderson, The Rain King	(146)
ARNOLD BENNETT	
Anna of the Five Towns	(144)
WILLIAM BLAKE	
Songs of Innocence, Songs of Experience	(173)
ROBERT BOLT	
A Man For All Seasons	(51)
ANNE BRONTË	
The Tenant of Wildfell Hall	(238)
CHARLOTTE BRONTË	
Jane Eyre	(21)
EMILY BRONTË	
Wuthering Heights	(43)
ROBERT BROWNING	
Men and Women	(226)
JOHN BUCHAN	
The Thirty-Nine Steps	(89)
JOHN BUNYAN	
The Pilgrim's Progress	(231)
GEORGE GORDON, LORD BYRON	
Selected Poems	(244)
ALBERT CAMUS	
L'Etranger (The Outsider)	(46)
GEOFFREY CHAUCER	
Prologue to the Canterbury Tales	(30)
The Franklin's Tale	(78)
The Knight's Tale	(97)
The Merchant's Tale	(193)
The Miller's Tale	(192)
The Nun's Priest's Tale	(16)
The Pardoner's Tale	(50)
The Wife of Bath's Tale	(109)
Troilus and Criseyde	(198)

	Series number
ANTON CHEKHOV	
The Cherry Orchard	(204)
SAMUEL TAYLOR COLERIDGE	
Selected Poems	(165)
WILKIE COLLINS	
The Moonstone	(217)
The Woman in White	(182)
SIR ARTHUR CONAN DOYLE	
The Hound of the Baskervilles	(53)
WILLIAM CONGREVE	
The Way of the World	(207)
JOSEPH CONRAD	
Heart of Darkness	(152)
Lord Jim	(150)
Nostromo	(68)
The Secret Agent	(138)
Youth and *Typhoon*	(100)
BRUCE DAWE	
Selected Poems	(219)
DANIEL DEFOE	
A Journal of the Plague Year	(227)
Moll Flanders	(153)
Robinson Crusoe	(28)
CHARLES DICKENS	
A Tale of Two Cities	(70)
Bleak House	(183)
David Copperfield	(9)
Great Expectations	(66)
Hard Times	(203)
Little Dorrit	(246)
Nicholas Nickleby	(161)
Oliver Twist	(101)
Our Mutual Friend	(228)
The Pickwick Papers	(110)
EMILY DICKINSON	
Selected Poems	(229)
JOHN DONNE	
Selected Poems	(199)
THEODORE DREISER	
Sister Carrie	(179)
GEORGE ELIOT	
Adam Bede	(14)
Silas Marner	(98)
The Mill on the Floss	(29)
T. S. ELIOT	
Four Quartets	(167)
Murder in the Cathedral	(149)
Selected Poems	(155)
The Waste Land	(45)
GEORGE FARQUHAR	
The Beaux Stratagem	(208)
WILLIAM FAULKNER	
Absalom, Absalom!	(124)
As I Lay Dying	(44)
Go Down, Moses	(163)
The Sound and the Fury	(136)
HENRY FIELDING	
Joseph Andrews	(105)
Tom Jones	(113)

Series number

JOHN OSBORNE
Look Back in Anger (128)

ALAN PATON
Cry, The Beloved Country (213)

THOMAS LOVE PEACOCK
Nightmare Abbey and *Crotchet Castle* (240)

HAROLD PINTER
The Birthday Party (25)
The Caretaker (106)

ALEXANDER POPE
Selected Poems (194)

THOMAS PYNCHON
The Crying of Lot 49 (148)

SIR WALTER SCOTT
Ivanhoe (58)
Quentin Durward (54)
The Heart of Midlothian (141)
Waverley (122)

PETER SHAFFER
The Royal Hunt of the Sun (170)

WILLIAM SHAKESPEARE
A Midsummer Night's Dream (26)
Antony and Cleopatra (82)
As You Like It (108)
Coriolanus (35)
Cymbeline (93)
Hamlet (84)
Henry IV Part I (83)
Henry IV Part II (140)
Henry V (40)
Julius Caesar (13)
King Lear (18)
Love's Labour's Lost (72)
Macbeth (4)
Measure for Measure (33)
Much Ado About Nothing (73)
Othello (34)
Richard II (41)
Richard III (119)
Romeo and Juliet (64)
Sonnets (181)
The Merchant of Venice (107)
The Taming of the Shrew (118)
The Tempest (22)
The Winter's Tale (65)
Troilus and Cressida (47)
Twelfth Night (42)
The Two Gentlemen of Verona (206)

GEORGE BERNARD SHAW
Androcles and the Lion (56)
Arms and the Man (12)
Caesar and Cleopatra (57)
Candida (247)
Major Barbara (195)
Pygmalion (5)
Saint Joan (237)

MARY SHELLEY
Frankenstein (248)

PERCY BYSSHE SHELLEY
Selected Poems (214)

RICHARD BRINSLEY SHERIDAN
The School for Scandal (55)
The Rivals (104)

WOLE SOYINKA
The Lion and the Jewel (158)
The Road (133)
Three Short Plays (172)

Series number

JOHN STEINBECK
Of Mice and Men (23)
The Grapes of Wrath (7)
The Pearl (99)

LAURENCE STERNE
A Sentimental Journey (241)

ROBERT LOUIS STEVENSON
Kidnapped (90)
Treasure Island (48)
Dr Jekyll and Mr Hyde (132)

TOM STOPPARD
Professional Foul (242)
Rosencrantz and Guildenstern are Dead (222)

JONATHAN SWIFT
Gulliver's Travels (61)

JOHN MILLINGTON SYNGE
The Playboy of the Western World (111)

ALFRED, LORD TENNYSON
Selected Poems (243)

W. M. THACKERAY
Vanity Fair (19)

DYLAN THOMAS
Under Milk Wood (197)

EDWARD THOMAS
Selected Poems (251)

FLORA THOMPSON
Lark Rise to Candleford (245)

J. R. R. TOLKIEN
The Hobbit (121)
The Lord of the Rings (230)

CYRIL TOURNEUR
The Revenger's Tragedy (215)

MARK TWAIN
Huckleberry Finn (49)
Tom Sawyer (76)

VIRGIL
The Aeneid (223)

VOLTAIRE
Candide (81)

EVELYN WAUGH
Decline and Fall (178)
A Handful of Dust (224)

JOHN WEBSTER
The Duchess of Malfi (171)
The White Devil (176)

H. G. WELLS
The History of Mr Polly (86)
The Invisible Man (52)
The War of the Worlds (103)

ARNOLD WESKER
Chips with Everything (184)
Roots (164)

PATRICK WHITE
Voss (190)

OSCAR WILDE
The Importance of Being Earnest (75)

TENNESSEE WILLIAMS
The Glass Menagerie (187)

VIRGINIA WOOLF
To the Lighthouse (162)

WILLIAM WORDSWORTH
Selected Poems (196)

Series number

F. SCOTT FITZGERALD
Tender is the Night (232)
The Great Gatsby (8)

E. M. FORSTER
A Passage to India (151)
Howards End (220)

ATHOL FUGARD
Selected Plays (63)

JOHN GALSWORTHY
Strife (239)

MRS GASKELL
North and South (60)

WILLIAM GOLDING
Lord of the Flies (77)
The Inheritors (209)

OLIVER GOLDSMITH
She Stoops to Conquer (71)
The Vicar of Wakefield (79)

ROBERT GRAVES
Goodbye to All That (249)

GRAHAM GREENE
Brighton Rock (202)
The Power and the Glory (188)

THOMAS HARDY
Far from the Madding Crowd (174)
Jude the Obscure (6)
Selected Poems (169)
Tess of the D'Urbervilles (80)
The Mayor of Casterbridge (39)
The Return of the Native (20)
The Trumpet Major (74)
The Woodlanders (160)
Under the Greenwood Tree (129)

L. P. HARTLEY
The Go-Between (36)
The Shrimp and the Anemone (123)

NATHANIEL HAWTHORNE
The Scarlet Letter (134)

ERNEST HEMINGWAY
A Farewell to Arms (145)
For Whom the Bell Tolls (95)
The African Stories (201)
The Old Man and the Sea (11)

GEORGE HERBERT
Selected Poems (233)

HERMANN HESSE
Steppenwolf (135)

BARRY HINES
Kes (189)

ANTHONY HOPE
The Prisoner of Zenda (88)

GERARD MANLEY HOPKINS
Selected Poems (205)

WILLIAM DEAN HOWELLS
The Rise of Silas Lapham (175)

RICHARD HUGHES
A High Wind in Jamaica (17)

THOMAS HUGHES
Tom Brown's Schooldays (2)

ALDOUS HUXLEY
Brave New World (156)

HENRIK IBSEN
A Doll's House (85)
Ghosts (131)
Hedda Gabler (210)

Series number

HENRY JAMES
Daisy Miller (147)
The Europeans (120)
The Portrait of a Lady (117)
The Turn of the Screw (27)
Washington Square (234)

SAMUEL JOHNSON
Rasselas (137)

BEN JONSON
The Alchemist (102)
Volpone (15)

JAMES JOYCE
Dubliners (250)

JOHN KEATS
Selected Poems (211)

RUDYARD KIPLING
Kim (114)

D. H. LAWRENCE
Sons and Lovers (24)
The Rainbow (59)
Women in Love (143)

CAMARA LAYE
L'Enfant Noir (191)

HARPER LEE
To Kill a Mocking-Bird (125)

LAURIE LEE
Cider with Rosie (186)

THOMAS MANN
Tonio Kröger (168)

CHRISTOPHER MARLOWE
Doctor Faustus (127)
Edward II (166)

ANDREW MARVELL
Selected Poems (235)

W. SOMERSET MAUGHAM
Of Human Bondage (185)
Selected Short Stories (38)

J. MEADE FALKNER
Moonfleet (221)

HERMAN MELVILLE
Billy Budd (10)
Moby Dick (126)

THOMAS MIDDLETON
Women Beware Women (236)

THOMAS MIDDLETON *and* WILLIAM ROWLEY
The Changeling (212)

ARTHUR MILLER
Death of a Salesman (32)
The Crucible (3)

JOHN MILTON
Paradise Lost I & II (94)
Paradise Lost IV & IX (87)
Selected Poems (177)

V. S. NAIPAUL
A House for Mr Biswas (180)

SEAN O'CASEY
Juno and the Paycock (112)
The Shadow of a Gunman (200)

GABRIEL OKARA
The Voice (157)

EUGENE O'NEILL
Mourning Becomes Electra (130)

GEORGE ORWELL
Animal Farm (37)
Nineteen Eighty-four (67)